# LEADERSHIP IN ACTION

## A HANDBOOK FOR LEADERSHIP

Ashley Goldsworthy

First published by Dog Ear Publishing
4010 W. 86th Street, Ste H
Indianapolis, IN 46268
www.dogearpublishing.net

ISBN: 978-159858-979-5

This book is printed on acid-free paper.

Printed in the United States of America

This book is dedicated to Shirley Anne Monica, who has given me her unconditional and total support, encouragement and love through 51 years as my wife and soulmate. I love her dearly and without her I would have achieved nothing.

# CONTENTS PAGE

# PREFACE

This is a book about people, about getting people to do what you want them to do, even when they might be inclined to do otherwise. It is about encouraging, convincing, exhorting, motivating and generally getting human beings to do something they would not have done without your intervention.

Leadership is a process. It is not a set of characteristics, it is not charisma, it is not a position, it is not a role. It is a process—a process involving people. It is about those who lead and those who are led. It is about those who challenge and those who accept. It is also about helping people to achieve their goals as well, both as individuals and groups. People often have a rough idea of what they want to achieve, but are unsure as to how to go about it. They need that sense of direction, that push in the back to get going, that confidence in themselves that they can do what they want to do.

Whilst I do not want to concentrate solely on business, nevertheless it is an important arena for the application of leadership, and it is the arena that will attract most of our attention in this book. Moreover, it will be mainly at the senior levels, as this is where my personal experience lies.

It is particularly important for Australia in this context. With the increasing globilisation of business, the advent of e-commerce, mega mergers, increased shareholder activity, and the continual redefining of business goals, strong business leadership is critical. And for Australia, with few companies straddling the globe, we face the danger of becoming a business backwater without the drive of dynamic leadership, not only in business, but also in government and research.

It would seem to be unnecessary to question the importance of people in business and yet one only has to look at the way many businesses are run to realise that the "people are our greatest asset" phrase, much used in annual reports, is nothing more than an empty cliché in far too many instances. Put very simply, people are the most important asset of any business, because they are the organisation's only sustainable competitive advantage.

# CHAPTER 1 -
# Of Geese and Broccoli

*Develop a Sense of Urgency in Everything you do.*

## The Geese

If you have ever watched a flock of geese fly overhead, you will have noticed that they fly in a V formation. Many years ago, a goose mathematician worked out that by so doing they would get 30% more lift and 71% more distance.

If one is going to travel long distances, as migrating geese do, it is obviously helpful to gain altitude to increase the probability of getting better winds. Needless to say, there is a significant benefit in gaining 71% more distance without expending extra resources. Ever since learning these advantages, they have organised themselves in this fashion when setting out on a long journey.

The V formation also thrusts one of the geese into what the army would call the "point" position. The one out front who chooses the path or direction the flock should follow. The leader has a very clear idea of where the flock wants to go and leads them in the right direction. Being in front means taking the knocks and buffeting of the wind. It means facing the challenge of unexpected events, like an F18 suddenly appearing on your port wing. It means having to keep up the pace without the benefit of the slipstream of a bird in front.

Inevitably the one in front gets tired and has to retire. The geese do this before they get to the stage where they can no longer keep up. They retire to a position further back in the flock where they can benefit from the efforts of a new leader. Interestingly, the decision to do this is taken by the leader at what they judge to be the appropriate time. If the decision is not taken at the appropriate time, it sees the leader depart the flock because they can no longer keep up.

How refreshing to have leaders who know when to retire and do so while they are still able to make a useful contribution to the group. Without inter-ruption, debate or discussion, the succession plan comes into play and a new leader immediately takes over. The newcomer also knows the direction in which the group is heading, because before starting out there had been a very detailed briefing session.

Everyone in the group knew the longitude, latitude, air speed, wind speed and direction, and ETA of the flight. The communication had been com-prehensive and care was taken to make sure that everyone had a very clear understanding of what was planned.

Effective communication is an important feature of the geese flight. We all know how vital it is that everyone is at all times conversant with the over-all direction and strategy of the group. Leaders need to know that the mem-bers of the team are united behind them.

The geese have developed a sophisticated method of wireless communica-tion called "honking", which enables them to do this in flight. If you have seen a flock of geese overhead, you will also have heard them. Their cease-less honking keeps all and sundry well informed of the flock's progress and the leader is constantly reassured by the audible communication behind him. I am often struck by the fact that many people think that by looking in the mirror they see a leader. What they need to realise is that if there is no one else in the mirror, they are not leading. One cannot be a leader without followers. It is not a solo role. It may be solitary, lonely, friendless, isolated or whatever, but it is not solo.

As inevitably happens from time to time, one of the geese, for whatever rea-son, finds the pace too hot and is unable to keep up. As the stricken bird falls behind, two geese stay with the stricken one, giving succor and com-fort, and determining whether there is any hope of recovery and rejoining the flock. If the consulting geese are of the mind that there is no hope, they will leave the stricken bird and rejoin the flock. However, they do not take that decision lightly and will remain with their stricken brethren until their own chance of catching up to the flock is at risk.

And finally the V formation has another purpose. One of the defining characteristics of leadership is vision, the clear and untrammeled understanding of the long-term outcome that is desired. The beacon on the hill, as it were, we are heading towards. So the geese, in their wisdom, fly in a V formation to indicate that they recognise very clearly the importance of vision.

We can learn many valuable leadership lessons from the geese:

> To have a clear sense of direction.
> To know where you are headed.
> To communicate constantly with your followers.
> To communicate clearly and unequivocally to your team.
> To make sure all the team understands your objective.
> To lead from the front.
> To care for the well being of your followers.
> To retire before it is too late.
> To conserve resources and reduce effort (costs).
> To maintain physical well being.
> To reward the achievers.
> To understand the need for sustained effort.
> To understand the importance of Vision.

## The Broccoli

So what of the broccoli? Look at a bunch of broccoli and you see a certain repetitive pattern. Break it into smaller pieces and you still see the same pattern repeated. It is the plant equivalent of a fractal, each part of which has the same geometry or statistical character as the whole.

The message here is that leadership is not something that occurs only at the top of an organisation. It is not just the 5-star general, the Pope, the president, or the CEO. It is something that can happen at any level in an organisation. As you go down through the organisation in the same way as you break down the broccoli, you face the same challenges, the same opportunities, to exercise leadership, albeit on a different scale.

As much as the Great Man theory of leadership prevalent in the early part of the 20th century has been discarded, so too has the idea that leadership is something exercised only at the peak of the organisational pyramid.

## Universality of Leadership

Leadership is universal. We have all experienced it throughout our lives, from our earliest years as children. Many of us will have exercised it, perhaps not always aware that we are doing so. It is this universality of leadership which in many ways helps to make it not only an important, but also a fascinating subject.

Leadership cannot be practised in a vacuum. It is not something you can practise by just knowing the theory. Experience is very important. It is like riding a pushbike. You can read all the books in the world on how to ride a bike, and have all the explanations and demonstrations in the world, but until you actually try to ride a bike, you are not going to learn how to actually do it.

I cannot teach you leadership and I cannot teach you to be leaders, so I do not pretend to do so. However, what you can do is learn about leadership. And you can learn to be leaders. Sure, there are natural abilities that may make you a better leader, but as you will learn from reading this book, that is also a little dangerous, as leaders, even great leaders, come in all shapes and sizes, all ages and race, men and women, and with an infinite diversity of skills, experience and backgrounds. There is no one mould for "the leader". Some believe the only school you learn leadership from is the school of hard knocks. Acknowledging that experience can be a valuable learning experience does not exclude other avenues. Formal study can usefully complement experience.

Leadership develops significantly through experience, but this can be very usefully complemented by the academic study of leadership. It should be obvious that the more you understand of human nature, the more you understand about effective communication, the more you understand how people work as teams, the more you understand motivation, and so on, the better leader you will be.

I mentioned above the universality of leadership. There are very few activities in this life where leadership is not important. That does not mean that everybody can be, or should want to be, a leader. But for those of you who do have a vision of things you want to achieve, leadership is going to play a major role in that pursuit.

## Some Myths

At this early stage, we should rid ourselves of some of the myths of leadership; otherwise, we will be tempted down the wrong path.

A common myth is that leadership is just commonsense. There is nothing special about leading, other than acting in the same manner as any person with common sense. But what is that? How do we know what that mythical person would do in every circumstance? What are the yardsticks and benchmarks for this common sense? In everyday usage, what we normally mean is to not do something silly. But this is no guide, because "silly" is a very subjective judgment. Most people probably thought the first pilots were silly. Today, lots of people think that bungee jumping is crazy , but obviously others do not.

When we are away from our loved ones, common sense says, "Absence makes the heart grow fonder." But common sense also says, "Out of sight, out of mind." These statements are, of course, contradictory— so much for common sense. If common sense were so easy to identify, we would bundle it up and share it with everybody.

An even more common myth is that leaders are born, not made. In other words, your destiny is sealed from the moment of birth. You will have the capacities, skills, knowledge and experience to lead nations, armies, churches, or business built into your genes. A glance at history shows the flaw in this assertion. People often grow in the face of challenge as they do with experience.

Vince Lombardi, the great American football coach, had it right- "Leaders aren't born they are made. And they are made just like anything else, through hard work. And that's the price we'll have to pay to achieve that goal, or any goal."

## Practice Not Theory

This volume does not pretend to be a scholarly tome in the sense of every second sentence being referenced by a bevy of footnotes, nor with a bibliography including everything ever written on leadership. In instances where quotes, ideas, and themes perhaps should have been attributed and were not, I apologise. It was done without malice and in the intent to enable an uninterrupted focus by the reader on the message rather than as a text-book.

What it sets out to do is to give a perspective based on 50 years of observation and experience in a variety of fields. It is both anecdotal and auto-biographical. It does not have to be read from cover to cover. You can open it at any page and hopefully learn something useful.

I have always encouraged people, particularly staff who worked with me, to take every opportunity to broaden their experience. It does not really matter in what field you get it. What it does is give you the opportunity to deal with different and perhaps novel problems, you meet new people and often people with different sets of values, you frequently have to operate within an unfamiliar context, and you oftentimes have to apply ill-defined and per-plexing criteria.

In this context I have had the good fortune to be able to do this myself, and hence my views are coloured by having observed and experienced leader-ship from the inside at the highest levels in the public sector, business, pol-itics, education, technology, the arts, and professional associations.

I believe understanding is enhanced by personal experience and it adds another dimension to observation. I spent many years as CEO of billion dollar businesses in banking, insurance, construction, and property devel-opment, including the invaluable challenge of starting a business from inception. This gave me the opportunity to see leadership from the board-room to the factory floor.

After having spent the beginnings of my working life in the public sector and seeing the machinations of the bureaucracy, it was an interesting change to move into the private sector, especially at a senior level. Leader-ship in the public sector is certainly a world apart from the private sector, although there are many common characteristics.

I was Federal President of the Liberal Party (1990-1993), one of the two major political parties in Australia, which has been in government at the national level for 42 of the 64 years since it was formed in 1944. In that arena it was fascinating to be a member of the Federal Executive of the Party for some 13 years during a period (1986-1999) in both opposition and government; a time during which there were several dramatic changes of leaders (i.e. the leader of the Federal Parliamentary Party).

On the day my (first) retirement from business was announced, I received an offer which had never entered my mind. This led me to embark on what turned out to be one of the most challenging and enjoyable periods of my working life: seven years at Australia's first private university.

Seven years (1990-1997) as Professor of Leadership and Dean of a School of Business provided a chance to experience an environment vastly different from the business world. In addition, it gave me the opportunity to help students learn about leadership. One cannot teach leadership, but one can teach students how to learn about leadership.

Those in business are fond of referring to those in academia as being in the "ivory tower" and themselves and being in the "real world". The cloisters of academia are as real as the world of business, but they are very different, and I doubt if the inhabitants of either realise just how different. There is much truth in the adage that university politics are so vicious because the issues are so trivial.

Somewhat related in the educational arena is my experience with the Business/Higher Education Round Table (B-HERT), which I helped found in 1990 when I was a member of the Business Council of Australia (a group of Australia's 100 largest companies) and Chairman of its Education & Training Committee. This body (B-HERT), which at various times has had sister bodies in the U.S., Canada, Japan, Poland, U.K. and elsewhere, has as its members the vice-chancellors of Australia's universities, business leaders, and the CEOs of major public research organisations. Its mission is to create more effective collaboration between big business and higher education for the benefit of the nation.

The opportunity to serve as president (elected and unpaid) and CEO (appointed and paid) of this body over a period of eleven years (1997-2008) and its unique membership of leaders in academia, business and research, has provided a rich tapestry of experience in many respects.

Professional associations present a unique set of conditions for those harbouring leadership ambitions. One distinctive feature is that you are amongst a group of equals. Sure there may be some that for one reason or another tend to stand out from the crowd, but in essence the playing field is relatively level, and certainly orders of magnitude more so than in business, politics or academia. Another distinctive feature from a leadership perspective is that there is quite a different type of power base to be established. The general absence of a stable elected hierarchy combined with a permanent secretariat presents a challenge for the aspiring leader.

My experience in this arena was primarily in information technology where I was president of the national society i.e. elected, on three occasions, separated by a decade, and also elected (1983) World President of the International Federation for Information Processing (IFIP). This latter role had an interesting aspect in that I was the first president (and still am one of only two) from the southern hemisphere. Uniquely, I also served for over four years as the CEO (appointed paid official) of the national association. This experience from both sides of the table provides a unique perspective on the handling of issues.

A somewhat related arena is that of learned academies, which enjoy a much higher status than professional associations. In Australia there are four such academies: science, humanities, social sciences, and technological sciences and engineering. I belong to the latter. These are different from the professional associations in that membership is by nomination (one cannot apply) and election by existing members, rather than by application and admission by meeting specified eligibility criteria. This tends to create an even more level playing field, as election by peers tends to be self-sustaining in the application of judgement rather than measurable criteria such as university degrees. In a leadership context, it also creates a unique climate.

The performing arts present another world. Whilst never being a performer, I was privileged over a period of 20 years to serve as chairman or member of the board of ballet, theatre and circus arts companies. Motivation, commitment, and dedication are part of the armoury of leadership. As a group, performing artists exhibit these characteristics to the extreme. Add sacrifice, and leadership aspirants have a mix that is both malleable and difficult.

I think it is important for the reader to be able to appreciate the background from which I am coming in relation to whatever views I have with respect to leadership. It is always dangerous to formulate opinions based on narrow experience and looking in from the outside.I hope that the brief outline of my background indicates that at least I have had the opportunity to see things in a variety of situations with a wide diversity of people, circumstances and issues.

In addition to the above, I have of course drawn extensively on the written material and authors listed in the bibliography. I have tried to extract from those writings the essence of the issues which I see as important in understanding the nature and exercise of leadership.

## An Australian Flavour

The book has a distinctly Australian flavour and this is quite intentional. It is the arena I know and the messages, if there are any, are directed to my home turf.

There are those who would say that too many Australian companies have chairmen and CEOs who are managers rather than leaders. For example, the Karpin report made this observation. Their U.S. counterparts are more often seen as leaders. Perhaps this is why in recent years in Australia, some of our largest companies (Westpac, AMP, BHP, Telstra, Suncorp, Mincom, ANZ, NAB) have seen it necessary to appoint CEOs from overseas, predominantly from the U.S. Why is this? At first blush, the Australian and U.S. business scenes may appear to be very similar, but there are some distinct differences, none more so than at the top of the company. The first difference that many people would identify is the pay scales, although of recent years the disparity is lessening. But more fundamental than this is the *modus operandi.*

In his book Paid to Decide, John Foden, global chairman of UK-based PA Consulting Group , says the CEO is paid to decide and that strategy is to make things happen (*The Australian Financial Review*, 15-16 April, 2000). When one looks at what the imported CEOs mentioned above have done following their appointment, this observation holds very true.

Alex Harris, president of the Australian-New Zealand American Chamber of Commerce of Chicago from 1993 until 1997, came back to Australia as managing director of the Masterstroke Group Pty. Ltd., she says (*The Australian Financial Review*, 15-16 April, 2000) Australian CEOs spend a third of their time in meetings and on committees where few decisions are actually made. She says they spend long hours examining what happened last week, last month, last quarter and last year, analysing what was done rather than using the information to decide what could be done. Yet, speed is everything. Compared with the American *modus operandi,* Australian CEOs often seem paralysed when it comes to decision-making. Information is meaningless if it is not used to change, to improve, to build upon, to act on.

Alan Jackson seems to agree. Jackson is one of Australia's best-known business leaders. He took the reins of a small company in 1977 and turned it into Australia's largest industrial company, BTR Nylex. In 1991, he landed the top job in London as the CEO of the global BTR operation. He came back to Australia as executive chairman of Austrim Ltd. He says: "Decision-making is an essential element to successful management. You can have all the expert advisers in the world and be armed with all the facts and figures to support a particular idea, but at the end of the day it is the CEO's decision to make, and succeed or fail. It is upon his shoulders the weight of responsibility falls." (*The Australian Financial Review*, 15-16 April, 2000). Unfortunately, his experience with Austrim was not as successful as his time with BTR.

If you look at very successful companies like GE, it is apparent that divisional managers are given the latitude, encouragement and performance targets to get on with the game. The responsibility is placed on the leader of that unit to get creative and come up with the desired result, or the division is sold or closed. At the same time they are being groomed for the top job. Had Australian companies such as BHP, AMP, Westpac, Telstra and so on done the same, perhaps we would not have needed so many overseas imports.

Part of the problem is delegation, or more precisely the failure to delegate. Australian CEOs pride themselves on being "hands-on" and Australian boards too often descend into management (meetings every 20 working days tends to encourage this). Many CEOs see it as a weakness to admit at a board meeting that they do not know the answer to every question the board might ask them. What they should be doing is making it clear that the role of CEO has very clear responsibilities and they are well on top of those, and that does not include being the chief expert on finance, human resources, marketing, sales, manufacturing, distribution and everything else that goes on in the company.

One clear illustration of this attitude and approach is the frequency of board meetings in Australia. With very few exceptions, major companies in Australia hold board meetings every month. If one accepts that the role of the board is to approve strategy, monitor performance, provide good governance, and protect stakeholder interests, it is nonsense to meet every 20 working days. Good corporate governance does not need this and in fact it is deleterious to good performance, because inevitably the board, with meetings so frequent, delves into detail it should not be concerned with, but it leaves directors with a warm fuzzy feeling that they are an indispensable part of the company and justifies their increasingly large directors' fees..

One only has to look at the appalling performance in recent years of the boards of some of our major companies to seek stark evidence of this. In fact, one has to wonder in some instances just what the board was doing at its frequent get-togethers to allow the company to get into such a mess.

On the other hand, most of the very large and successful companies in the US have far less frequent board meetings and delegate much more to management. Companies such as GE have four board meetings a year. GE has a capitalization greater than the top 100 companies in Australia combined, but to suggest quarterly board meetings to our 'blue chips' would cause long and hearty derision.

There are very few Australian major corporates that operate like this. Don Mercer, Chairman of the Australian Institute of Company Directors, Chairman of Orica and former CEO of the ANZ bank, clearly sympathises with this view. He is reported as saying, "Non-executive directors contribute precious little to listed companies and public expectations of what they can do are unrealistic. The typical non-executive director of an Australian listed company spends 250 hours on the job or about three days a month. These are people who are part-time and increasingly non-expert because they have to be independent. The contribution of directors is at best advisory, helpful and all those good things, but they are (at annual general meetings) up on a stage saying "thank you, thank you". (*The Australian Financial Review*, 29 April 2004, p.7)

This book is a combination of theory, practical experience, observation, anecdotal evidence, hearsay, personal opinion and bias, all designed to help those who would lead do so more effectively. As John Kennedy was going to say in a speech he was to deliver on the day he was assassinated in Dallas, "Leadership and learning are indispensable to each other."

# CHAPTER 2 -

# Mobilisation—Leaders, Shepherds, Entrepreneurs, Managers

*He who swims against the tide will never be swept out to sea.*

## Not One But Several

I subtitled this book *A Handbook for Leadership* (not *Leaders*) for a very specific reason. The clue is in the title of this chapter. Whilst we are discussing a process we shall call leadership, we need to understand that there are complementary processes that are similar to, but at the same time, different from what we call leadership. It is important to understand the differences. These processes overlap in many respects. They are all concerned with people. They are all concerned with striving to achieve specific goals or outcomes.

The best word I can think of to cover the four categories is mobilisation. It has military overtones, but it does describe the basic thrust of the four activities—to organise and move a group of people towards a defined outcome. There are at least four distinct and different types of people and types of processes involved in mobilisation. There are leaders, there are shepherds, there are entrepreneurs, and there are managers. There has been much written about the difference between leadership and management, and several authors have documented what they see as the differences. One of the best known is by Bennis (Bennis, 1989), and much of what he suggests is included in my table below.

Entrepreneurs warrant a category of their own. Whilst they share many of the characteristics of leaders, they do have attributes which place them and the process apart. I have tried to identify some of those attributes in the table.

There is another group of mobilisers who are much more than 'senior managers' and who could be categorised as 'deputy leaders'. They are more concerned with change than are managers, but they are not prepared to actively seek change as are leaders. Nor do they relish the chaos and ambiguity that are the lifeblood of leaders. These are the people, and all of us can bring to mind those we know, who are often regarded as the ideal or perfect deputy, but it is widely recognised that, for whatever reason, they are not leaders. I have called this category "shepherds". Again, whilst there is some overlap with the other categories, I believe there is enough difference to warrant their own category.

It needs to be emphasised that a person does not have to be one or the other of these categories. Most of us have a bit of all of them in us. It is the proportion of the mix that is the critical issue. It is also important to realise that one does not "switch" from one category to another, as one would change clothes. These are not precisely defined and neatly bounded profiles or behaviour patterns. They are a mixture of complex and ever varying patterns of behaviour and characteristics, which will almost invariably be a soup of the attributes in the table of varying proportions.

The nature of the mix is what categorises the person and the process as leading, shepherding, managing or entrepreneuring. I am not suggesting in any way that any one category is more important than another , as they are all important in their place. There are situations when it is far more important to be an effective manager than a leader, and the reverse also applies— similarly with the other categories. However, it is important to recognise that there are specific attributes, actions and approaches that tend to categorise and define.

| LEADER | SHEPHERD | ENTREPRENEUR | MANAGER |
|---|---|---|---|
| Innovate | Sustain | Analyse | Administer |
| Develop | Maintain | Create | Maintain |
| Inspire | Encourage | Anything is Possible | Control |
| Long-term view | Today | Tomorrow | Short-term view |
| Ask What and Why | Ask Where | Ask Why Not | Ask How & When |
| Originate | Copy | Iconoclast | Imitate |
| Challenge status quo | Accept status quo | Ignore status quo | Accept status quo |
| Impatient | Stoic | Impatient | Unflustered |
| Welcome chaos | Avoid chaos | Invent chaos | Seek order |
| Focus on People | Focus on Care | Focus on Product/Service | Focus on Systems |
| Emotionally attuned | Sympathetic | Insensitive | Reactive |
| Eye on Horizon | Eye on Surroundings | Eye on Sales | Eye on Bottom Line |
| Do the Right Thing | Do the Easiest Thing | Does His Thing | Do Things Right |
| One of a Kind | One of Many | Unorthodox | Predictable |
| Challenges | Calm | Luck | Structure |
| Empowerment | Control | Tenacity | Power |
| Accept Risk | Avoid Risk | Calculated Risk | Reduce Risk |
| Creates Culture | Acknowledges Culture | Ignores Culture | Maintains Culture |
| Strategy | Tactics | Fruition | Process |
| Vision | Perception | Dream | Plan |
| Internal Control | External Control | Inner Locus of Control | External Control |
| Seeks Ambiguity | Avoids Ambiguity | Tolerates Ambiguity | Dislikes Ambiguity |

## Leadership

It is always useful to define what is being discussed and in respect to leadership there are as many definitions as there are authors. There is no one single definition of leadership despite, or perhaps, because there has been more written about leadership in the past 30 years than any other single topic in the social sciences. I am not criticising this fact, but merely underlining that there is no one single definition. There is no right or wrong answer. It is such a complex and involved concept that definitions tend to focus on the specific aspects which authors see as central to their thesis.

Leadership means different things to different people. This is not surprising, because there are literally infinite variations of the variables that interact in the leadership process and people view them and their relevance differently.

Impreciseness of the language is also another factor. We tend to use terms such as leadership, management, administration, supervision, authority, control, directing and so on to mean the same thing. We should also remember that many authors are exploring particular aspects or a particular view of leadership, and naturally their definition will reflect that approach. It would be foolish to do otherwise.

I do not want to spend a lot of time arguing a definition. I suspect most of us have a fairly clear idea of what we are talking about and fine variations are not that important. Paul Keating, when he was prime minister, had no doubt (which was not uncommon for him) that what was needed was leadership. Addressing the Labor Party National Conference in 1994, he said (*The Australian*, 27/9/94), "Labor had the courage, the love, the labour and the imagination to lead Australia into the 21st century. And I mean lead. I don't mean manage or re-arrange. I don't mean occupy time or space. I don't mean talk until the people of Australia stop listening."

What I will do is to give a number of definitions which will clearly demonstrate the points I am making. Hughes et al (1993, p.6) and Yukl (1994, p.2-3) give several:

1.  The creative and directive force of morale.
2.  The process by which an agent induces a subordinate to behave in a desired manner.
3.  The presence of a particular influence relationship between two or more persons.
4.  Directing and coordinating the work of group members.
5.  An interpersonal relation in which others comply because they want to, not because they have to.
6.  Transforming followers, creating visions of the goals that may be attained, and articulating for the followers the way to attain those goals.
7.  The process of influencing an organised group toward accomplishing its goals.
8.  Actions that focus resources to create desirable opportunities.
9.  The behaviour of an individual when he is directing the activities of a group toward a shared goal.
10. Interpersonal influence exercised in a situation, and directed, through the communication process, toward the attainment of a specified goal or goals.
11. The initiation and maintenance of structure in expectation and interaction.
12. The influential increment over and above mechanical compliance with the routine directives of the organisation.
13. A process of giving purpose (meaningful direction) to collective effort, and causing willing effort to be expended to achieve purpose.
14. Leaders are those who consistently make effective contributions to social order, and who are expected and perceived to do so.

Another definition I particularly like is that given by Colin Powell, the ex-Chairman of the Joint Chiefs of Staff and Secretary of State in the United States in his autobiography (Powell, 1995). "Leadership is the art of accomplishing more than the science of management says is possible." This definition raises a number of aspects we will discuss later.

It is useful to have a look at the various definitions to see the common elements as well as the differences. It also helps us to appreciate just how many factors affect leadership. Several of the definitions refer to "influence". This is certainly a central characteristic of leadership, and one I will be discussing later.

Other definitions imply different relationships between the leader and followers, from "subordinate" in #2, to "directing" in #4, "because they want to" in #5 (presumably excluding coercion), to "maintenance of structure" in #11. We see several references to "group members", "collective effort", "group" and "followers", underlining the essence of getting others to do something.

Whatever definition we adopt, for our purposes it must include the influencing of objectives and strategy, influencing the level of commitment of the followers to the task, and influencing the culture of the organisation. The latter, I believe, is a fundamental requirement of leadership and too often ignored. We shall therefore adopt a simple definition of leadership:

***The process of convincing a group of people to commit to do something they would not otherwise do.***

It is critical to emphasise the central concept in this definition is that leadership is a process. It is a process which involves the leader, the followers, and the situation. The process is the interaction between these three components. The outcome is leadership.

It is important to recognise the differences between the various outcomes—leadership, management, entrepreneurship, shepherding—to understand the nature of the various roles, and the characteristics and behaviours that are relevant. The difference is more than academic. It is critical in practice. It surprises me that the significance is so often ignored, not understood or just not seen as important.

The more perceptive business leaders do recognize the importance of the difference. Frank Blount, who was CEO of Telstra for almost seven years, said on one occasion (The AGE 12/11/98) just before he retired that he was struck by the difference between Australian managers and leaders. "I have observed this first-hand in Telstra, but I believe it exists more widely in this country. Certainly I hear CEOs of other companies voicing similar sentiments. I'm talking about effective mangers who react to change, but can't seem to proactively drive required change, who have no problem managing up and down in the traditional hierarchical model, but have not a clue about human networking at every level—vertically and horizontally—where the real value is." Blount is right. We have (in Australia) a management culture and not a leadership culture.

## Management

Managers are used to managing relations up and down the hierarchy. The vocabulary of "superior" and "subordinate" is their vernacular. Managing lateral relationships is foreign to them. Many managers do not seem to understand that they are there to support staff, not to direct and control them. The manager moves people as pieces on a chessboard. The leader moves people emotionally, to prepare them for change.

The aphorism I used in the heading of Chapter 1-Develop a Sense of Urgency in everything you do, is one of my fundamental beliefs. Those who have worked with me will be aware that my internal notepaper always had the same message, over the years and in different organisations. The message was (and always in red) "A Sense of Urgency". I always felt that one of the basic needs was for everybody to accept that tomorrow was another day and progress could not and would not wait. Managers actively seek to instill order, routine and predictability. Leaders are impatient and actively seek to destroy routine and predictability.

Management is, above all, rational and logical. It is subject to rigorous analysis, it is predictable, and it is about the containment of risk. The attitude to risk is a defining difference between leaders, managers and entrepreneurs. Leaders not only welcome the opportunity to take risks, they see risk-taking as an essential and natural part of leading. However, there is a caveat when it comes to the nature of the risk. Corporate leaders value their status and they will very rarely be too adventurous with that. Oftentimes the decision to invest or not invest shareholders' funds rests not so much on the

ROI (return on investment) as it does on ROS (return on status). Many, many projects are entered into because of corporate egotism. A recent example (June, 2005) is the decision by Multiplex to build the Wembley Stadium in London, which has turned out to be a financial disaster.

Another factor which sometimes enters the equation is competitive arrogance. The organisation feels so competent in its own abilities that it will pursue projects, because it believes no one else can, or will, want to do them. It then becomes oblivious to the costs and risks involved.

Entrepreneurs thrive on risk and often put at risk enormous slabs of their personal and family assets. They are prepared to risk all. The better ones do this in a calculated and calculating manner. They have assessed the odds and have come to a view as to the probability of their succeeding. They have assessed the risk-reward equation and are prepared to act accordingly. They would hotly deny they are being foolish or taking unnecessary risks. The manager finds this sort of behaviour incomprehensible. He sees no logic in taking unnecessary risks. Management can therefore be taught. Evidence the proliferation of Schools of Management at our universities (and the absence of Schools of Leadership).

The Industry Task Force on Leadership and Management Skills, chaired by David Karpin (hence the Karpin Report) in 1994, was very forthright on the lack of leadership skills in Australia and the predominance of management skills. Karpin said (*The Australian Financial Review,* 25 May 1994) that managers were not displaying the foresight, vision and flexibility which, along with technical and managerial skills, could inspire others around them to support a mission or an idea.

Research undertaken for the task force showed that Australian managers were weak on vision, decisiveness, teamwork and self-confidence, but rated well on hard work, honesty and egalitarianism. But the real message from the task force was that Australian managers were not operating as leaders. Karpin said, "Our enterprises and educators have achieved reasonable levels of competence in relation to planning, monitoring, control and co-ordination...However,...leaders and managers of the future, as well as the present, need to possess skills and attributes far beyond that... True leadership in the business sense involves creating a vision and inspiring those around you and working with you to strive to make that vision a reality."

Academic management, or more precisely management in academia, is like, as Donald Kennedy, ex-president of Stanford, put it: herding cats. The loyalty of most academics is to their worldwide colleagues in their discipline rather than to their institution—the university. Being an engineer, for example.

Being an academic is also a very individualistic calling. They sit most days in their offices working by themselves on research, writing or reading. Their main rewards are personal—publications, promotion—rather than organisational. Collaboration with colleagues in their own school or department is often minimal.

One of the great furphys of academia is that it is a collegiate environment. The image of brother academics walking arm-in-arm towards the intellectual horizon is pure fiction. I found business to be much more collegiate than academe. This is not necessarily a bad thing; it just needs to be recognised as part of the management challenge. In an institution where, in the words of John Henry Cardinal Newman (Newman, 1987, p.121), "Such is the constitution of the human mind, that any kind of knowledge, if it be really such, is its own reward", the use of performance measures and productivity indicators is unlikely to be effective.

The Vice-Chancellor of Australia's oldest university, Sydney University, Professor Gavin Brown, recognises this very well. In an article in The Australian on 11 September 1996, headed "Leadership the Key to Our Prosperity", he said, "By tradition vice-chancellors were ecclesiastical figureheads speaking for and from the college. Now we are also chief executives of massive public bureaucracies with multi-million-dollar turnovers. Of course we must work to develop strategic planning, to better our financial management and to mobilise our resources more effectively. But management in itself, is relatively easy—the real need is leadership. This country needs leadership of its universities and leadership by its universities."

In a nutshell, Brown not only pinpoints the importance of management, but the over-riding imperative of leadership. Nevertheless, we have to realise that organisations, and particularly businesses, have different needs at different times. It is rare for any organisation to be in a state of constant change and generally organisations need a blend of skills in different proportions at different times.

As a generalisation, most institutions need fewer leaders than they do managers or shepherds. If you doubt this, just imagine an organisation comprised solely of "leaders". Not a pretty thought. Perhaps this is fortuitous in the sense that business, and higher education for that matter, has become expert at developing managers and are still very amateurish at developing leaders.

Fortunately in today's environment, leadership is seen as much more sexy than management. And we are going to see even more emphasis on leadership in the period ahead. Leadership should be valued, but not at the expense of the other areas of mobilisation. What people are and what they do is generally rather different from what they perceive themselves as being and doing.

## Entrepreneurs

The previous comment of the differences between reality and perception is probably least evident in entrepreneurs. Entrepreneurs are generally driven by a desire for money, for success, and for freedom. Entrepreneurs see themselves as knights in armour taking on the world. The last thing that they would be prepared to do is work for someone else (although many, in fact, end up doing just this).

Risk is the real delineator between leaders, managers and entrepreneurs. The entrepreneur is the avid seeker of wealth, status and independence. An interesting question is whether entrepreneurs need or benefit from formal education. Does this rob them of their flair, their originality, and their innovativeness? The answer from academia is a resounding, No. Several universities in Australia run programs in entrepreneurship, which really focus on giving people the fundamental skills to establish a business and then survive. They try to remove from the equation failure due to lack of management skills.

The main reason why new firms fail is not because they have a bad product, but because of a lack of management skills. Teaching entrepreneurs how to formulate a business plan, what can be done to fund a new venture, what marketing is all about, how to manage risk, and so on, all helps to reduce the potential for failure.

When I chaired the *Information Industries Task Force* in 1997 for the Federal government, with the task of providing the government with a strategy for the development of the information industries in Australia, we met with hundreds of start-up companies. We got a series of very clear messages from those who were in early stages of building their empires.

Firstly, they said they were not "investor ready". They recognised they did not have the skills to put together the necessary business plan and other arguments to convince investors their new venture had any chance of success. These are skills that can be taught. Secondly, they said they were not "export ready". In other words, they knew that exporting their product or starting business in another country was much more than sending their product overseas or getting off a plane in London, opening an office, and declaring they were now international.

Again, there is a lot of information that can be provided to help entrepreneurs prepare themselves for setting up business in foreign countries. A special class of entrepreneurs is those with entrepreneurial spirit within large organisations, sometimes called intrapreneurs. They exhibit the characteristics of entrepreneurs without having to risk their own assets in the venture. They can pursue high-risk ventures with shareholder funds. Whilst this may still expose them to some sort of risk in terms of their future career, this is a lot less painful than going bankrupt. In fact with the golden handshakes prevalent today, it may be positively wealth producing to be thrown out for failure. Certainly many CEOs in Australia today are being more than generously rewarded for turning in dismal and disappointing performances.

Encouraging intrapreneurs is another way of encouraging innovation in an organisation. I believe it is essential to encourage innovation, but this does entail a rethink of attitudes to failure in an organisation.

In the table above I said that entrepreneurs take "Calculated Risk", leaders "Accept Risk", shepherds "Avoid Risk", and managers "Reduce Risk". Therefore, a leader will have no problem encouraging intrapreneurs. On the other hand, shepherds and managers will have difficulty. CEOs who want to create more innovation and value within their own organisations need to be leaders. There are many adages which reinforce failure as a precursor to success: "You learn more from failure than you do from success"; "Failure is the stepping stone to success"; "Failure is not a way of life. It's only a moment in time. Get over it and move on!"

One view is that failures and mistakes are an index of organisational risk-taking. And it goes without saying that risk-taking is an essential characteristic of any company that wants to be entrepreneurial.

Somewhat allied with risk, but nevertheless different, is the issue of "uncertainty". What is the likely outcome? A total lack of failure would indicate that commercial decisions with genuine uncertainty are being avoided.

Westpac CEO David Morgan is reported (*The Australian Financial Review*, 4-5 February, 2006, p.16) as saying, "You want people to make mistakes—people who don't make mistakes probably aren't doing enough. We had an issue internally in the mid to late 1990's, that, as a result of reaction to mistakes in the 1980's, we became too risk-averse as a culture. So a lack of mistakes may, in fact, not be a good thing for the organisation—it can be a symptom of timidity."

Whilst a certain level of failure may be good for the organisation, individuals generally want nothing to do with it. This is a challenge for the leader, because he has to balance human nature, which does not like failure, or even admitting failure, with a recognition that most ideas fail. Winston Churchill once remarked that success was the ability to go from failure to failure without losing your enthusiasm.

Foster's former CEO Trevor O'Hoy says that, "…sometimes the things the organisation learns from a failed product provide some consolation. Our Empire lager brand was a good example: while it was a commercial flop, the fact that we had as an organisation, gone through the process of designing and launching a non-traditional beer had some value. I have no doubt that the success of subsequent products…was built on the earlier failure." (*The Australian Financial Review*, 4-5 February, 2006, p.16)

One has to be careful of the potential negative effect of persistence. I think persistence is a wonderful virtue, but you have to know when to cut your losses.

## Shepherds

An additional and new category which I am introducing into the schema of leadership is "shepherd". "Shepherds watch the flock by night" are the words of a Christmas carol, and there is definitely a distinctive type in the mobilisation arena that does not fit into the leadership, management, or entrepreneurship categories.

Who and what are shepherds? In some contexts they may be referred to as "caretakers". People who are seen to be holding the fort until a more permanent appointment can be made. I see shepherds as more than this. They have more than a caretaker role. In my experience I have seen people put into a potential leadership role, but they just fall short of what is needed. They want to do more than "control" as a manager, but they fail to "inspire" as leaders.

Whilst the manager may "imitate", the shepherd tends to "copy". The latter is different in the sense that the shepherd wants to move forward, but does not quite have the capacity to challenge the status quo as effectively as a leader would. Whilst the manager tries to introduce order into chaos, and the leader positively welcomes chaos, the shepherd tries to avoid it.

The leader sees people as his greatest asset and devotes considerable attention and effort to extract the best from them. Motivation, inspiration, exhortation and encouragement are the leader's tools of trade. Shepherds do not have the same level of energy or penetration. They certainly recognise the key role of people, more so than managers who tend to focus on process , so they tend to exercise a more caring role rather than an inspirational one.

The leader would have his troops up and over the barricades, the manager would have a detailed examination of the barricades before doing anything, the shepherd would see if his troops could go around the barricades, and the entrepreneur would attempt to blow them up.

# CHAPTER 3 -

# Vision

*Remember the next time is far more important than the last time.*

## The Plea

"Give us a CEO with Vision" was the plea of a letter to the Editor of the *The Australian Financial Review,* in which the outcome being sought was a stronger Australian dollar and the CEO in question was the Prime Minister. A leader without a vision is an oxymoron. Leaders need to have a very clear idea, notion, understanding of what they want to achieve. One cannot lead in circles, because that will inevitably become a whirlpool and suck in failure.

What is a vision? A vision is a realistic, credible, challenging, desirable future for an organisation. A vision needs to be energizing. It needs to generate excitement. It needs to foster commitment. It needs to feed the desire to succeed. It should enflame the passions. Visions are not a new concept. "Where there is no vision, the people perish." (Proverbs 29:18).

In the business world, some examples of exemplary visions are Henry Ford's vision of a widely affordable car; Steve Job's vision of a desktop computer for personal use; and Walt Disney's vision of Disneyland as a place for people to find happiness and knowledge.

I said a vision needs to be passionate. The best example I know is encapsulated in Martin Luther King's speech delivered on the steps of the Lincoln Memorial in Washington D.C. on 28 August, 1963; his famous "I Have a

Dream" speech. This is one of the most moving speeches I have ever read, and to listen to it delivered in his magnificent voice is to be transported into his dream. "When we let freedom ring, when we let it ring from every village and hamlet, from every state and every city, we will be able to speed up that day when all of God's children, black men and white men, Jews and Gentiles, Protestants and Catholics, will be able to join hands and sing in the words of the old Negro spiritual, "Free at last! Free at last! Thank God Almighty, we are free at last!"

Several common characteristics immediately leap out of these definitions. They all deal with the future. Vision is where tomorrow begins. They all conjure up clear images of the future that is being aimed at. They are all energising. They call forth the commitment, effort, and resources that will be necessary to achieve the goal. They are simple, uncomplicated messages. Make no mistake. Inspired leadership can transform organisations.

Under a heading "CEOs suffer vision deficit", the *The Australian Financial Review* (13 December 1999, p.4) reported on a survey of 500 senior executives in Australia which found that only 5.4 percent of senior executives (the followers) thought that their CEOs (the supposed leaders) were actively engaged in promoting future growth, and only 2.3 percent felt that their CEO was creating the climate for innovation and technological progress.

Most believed their CEOs were focused on day-to-day issues which did not lead to organisational longevity. That is management not leadership. Do not confuse leadership with strategy. Ford may well have had a vision for a widely affordable car, but there were a lot of decisions that had to be made as to what the vehicle would look like, how it would be powered, how it would be manufactured, how it would be sold, etc., etc., before his vision could be realised.

Strategies are the means to the end. The end is the vision. A leader's vision inevitably encapsulates their own personal values, what they want to achieve in life, and the sort of person they are. This means that the vision for the organisation may well be the same as the leader's personal vision. Never try to sell a vision that does not accord with your personal values.

There is an old Chinese proverb that says unless you change direction, you are likely to arrive at where you are headed. Leaders are totally results oriented. Their vision is a tool to motivate others to strive to achieve those very same results. This is why we need leaders. They get the organisation going.

A vision is a light shining on a faraway hill. It is a beacon showing where the organisation is going in the long term. It does not show all the valleys and hills that will have to be conquered to get there. It does not show the pathway of how to get there, but it should shine clearly for everyone in the organisation to see, so that they all know where they are going.

I do not want to dwell on semantics, but it is important to understand that a vision is not a Mission. We see these words bandied about with gay abandon and oftentimes incorrectly used. A Mission is the rationale of the organisation ; its reason for existence. The Mission of an organisation might be to build quality affordable houses. Its vision might be to be the largest house builder in Australia. To state that an organisation has a mission is to state its purpose, not its direction.

It might well be asked, *How do you create a vision*? Is it serendipity? Does one leap out of bed in the morning with a sudden awakening? Is it the result of long and detailed analysis and research? Does it suddenly come without warning? Just what does one do? What one has to do is ask a lot of questions. The first and most important question, in a business context is, *What business are we in*? This is the most fundamental question a leader can ask, and it should be asked every day. The answer to this question may be the difference between success and failure.

What business is McDonald's in? The world's largest hamburger chain? An international franchiser? The largest potato and beef processor in the world? A developer of prime retail sites? The business of customer service? Brett Godfrey, the CEO of Virgin Blue airline maintains that they are in the customer service business, not the airline business.

You need to question the purpose or mission of your organisation. You need to question the underlying values of your organisation. What is your organisation's unique position in the marketplace? What are the operating strengths and weaknesses of the operation? What is the current strategy and can it be defended? What is the culture?

Values affect vision in several ways. When you think of Jaguar, Volvo and Holden, they are all in the motor vehicle industry, but they all have different values and so they emphasise different qualities like design, safety and economy.

Visions need a regular reality check. Does the vision relate to the critical stakeholders in the organisation? And remember these stakeholders exist both within and without the organisation. Does the vision accord with the interests and expectations of the major stakeholders? What threats or opportunities emanate from these stakeholders? What boundaries are there to the vision? Are there time, geographical, financial, physical, or social constraints which may militate against the achievement of the vision? It is of little use having a vision if you do not know when the vision has been achieved?

Whilst a vision is about the future, it is not a forecast or a prediction. It is not a prophecy. A vision does not have to be factual. Whilst it needs a reality check, it does not deal with reality. It deals with possible and desirable futures. It is the reality of those that have to be assessed. It is full of speculations, assumptions, and value judgements. How real was it for Honda to say it was going to be the second Ford? A vision cannot be true or false. It is a desired future. A vision is not set in concrete. It should be regularly reviewed. Circumstances change and visions may need to change.

Edwin Land built the Polaroid company on a successful vision of an instantly developing film. However, when he tried to extend the vision to Polavision, an instant movie system, the company lost over US$250 million. By then video recorders had arrived and the home movie market virtually disappeared.

Sebastian Kreske had a vision at the turn of the 20th century of a chain of variety stores offering very low prices made possible by centralised control and purchasing. It was an excellent vision that brought prosperity until the early 1950's, when shopping centres, supermarkets, and large chains began to attract large numbers of the customers who bought at Kreske's.

A new vision was formulated that led to the K-Mart chain of discount department stores that was such a success that by 1975 Kreske was second only to Sears in general merchandising. But soon enough that vision was challenged by a wave of specialty retailers, warehouse clubs and regional discount chains like Wal-Mart that better met the needs of their local customers. Wal-Mart has now become one of the most successful retailers in the world.

Visions can be destroyed by changes beyond the organisation's control. For example, the asbestos industry was virtually eliminated by environmental regulations. The tobacco industry, particularly in Western countries, is fighting a rearguard action against medical research, health concerns, and government regulation.

The purpose of a vision is to inspire, encourage and enthuse. It should never be a constraint on actions except those inconsistent with the vision. It is designed to unleash energy not contain it, to open up opportunities rather than restrict them, and to serve as a catalyst for the changes needed to ensure the long-term success of the organisation.

One might ask what makes a good vision. After all, not just any vision will do. If leaders want to energise the troops, as they do, they have to find the right vision.

So what makes a good vision? Visions need to be idealistic. Unless a vision offers a new view of the future, it will not inspire or enthuse people. It will not set a new standard or attract commitment. It has to be demonstrably better for the organisation, for the people in it, and the society within which it operates. Walt Disney's vision is an example which meets these criteria.

Visions need to be appropriate for the organisation and the times. They have to set high standards of excellence and reflect high ideals. They have to be persuasive and credible. The latter may be a problem in that a vision almost by definition is "incredible". They have to inspire enthusiasm and encourage commitment. To do this they must be articulate and unambiguous. A vision loses its purpose if it is open to interpretation. It has to be crystal clear. Above all they must be ambitious. Striving for little is counter-productive. Visions should call for sacrifice and emotional investment by followers.

Unless a vision is widely shared it is an empty dream. A vision should be a force for change. Walt Disney, through his vision, almost single-handedly reinvented the idea of an amusement park. Over thirty years ago, Bill Gates, Microsoft's co-founder, set out a radical vision for the fledgling software company. That vision, aimed at part in motivating Microsoft's employees, was to help put a PC on every desk and in every home. Gates said, "You want the vision of a company to be breathtaking like 'wow, do you really think you can do that', and certainly in 1975 saying there would be a computer on every desk and in every home was beyond wild." (*Financial Times*, 3 November 1999) He said, "In fact we even suppressed the 'in every home' bit in presentations to business groups because it was so wild they would think we weren't serious about business computing."

Gates then went on to explain that whilst that vision had made incredible progress, even that breadth of vision did not encompass what was going on

then and so for the first time in their (then) 25 year history, they had
changed their vision statement to talk about empowering people in a
'broader fashion—any time, any place on any device'. Microsoft had a
vision statement that lasted for 25 years and it became necessary to change
it because it was no longer radical. He said, "That's not bad. Our new vision
statement is actually aimed more at the excitement of people building the
products at Microsoft more than anything else. The new vision is really an
extension; it's just more ambitious than the old. We needed to step up the
radical notion. Even though the PC is really the centre of it, we needed to
highlight the role of software. That is the key thing."

For those who might disparage the "vision thing", as an American President
once famously did, the above should be a sobering reflection of the power
a vision can have.

# CHAPTER 4 -

# Power and Influence

*If you think you are larger than life, look in the mirror.*

## The Difference

Power is reputedly an aphrodisiac. Power is defined in the Oxford Dictionary as, "the ability to do or act", so that is probably one of its pleasurable aspects. Power goes hand- in-hand with "influence", defined as the "effect a person has on another". Together power and influence are respectively the foundation and framework of the structure of leadership. Whilst it might be hand-in-hand, it is not necessarily nose-to-nose. One may be considerably "bigger" than the other. There exists a surprising amount of confusion between the two. Many people use them as synonyms, whereas they are quite different attributes. Leaders should be in no doubt as to the difference. It could be disastrous.

Julius Caesar had power; Calpurnia had influence, but not enough, unfortunately, at the critical time. Presidents of the United States have power. They can appoint Supreme Court judges, parcel out the federal budget and command armies, but their level of influence varies dramatically. In 1996, *Time* magazine did an article on power and influence and Bill Clinton ranked as the most powerful person in America, followed by Bill Gates, Alan Greenspan, Rupert Murdoch (CEO, News Corp.), Michael Eisner (CEO, Walt Disney Co.), Jack Welch (CEO, General Electric), Andrew Grove (CEO, Intel), Jack Smith (CEO, General Motors), Ned Johnson (CEO, Fidelity), and Newt Gingrich (Speaker of the House).

However, when it came to the most influential persons in America, Clinton, the acknowledged leader of the free world, could not qualify as one of the 25 most influential people in America. In analysing why, *Time* said he lacked those things that help define influence, "...a vision that inspires people to shed their doubts and follow his lead, an ability to connect with people and shape the way they look at the world."

Power without influence is a very blunt instrument. Power may make people do things the way you want them to, but that is not enough. You need influence to make them see things the way you do. It is interesting to note the preponderance of business leaders amongst the list.

Political and military leaders are generally perceived to exercise more power than business leaders (but I suspect Jesus and Mohammed leave them all behind). But the power of the latter (business) should not be underestimated, because they do sometimes exercise enormous power to influence the lives of many—employees, shareholders, suppliers, customers, whole communities and perhaps even governments.

Witness the effects in Australia in recent years of the decision of the major banks to close branches in small country towns, or the decision of BHP to close down the steelworks in Newcastle, or the decision of Toyota to close manufacturing in Adelaide. These sorts of decisions can have enormous ramifications on the lives of many people. We need to ask ourselves if there is a compromise between maximising the bottom line and in some way easing the burden on people. The rationalists will immediately protest that it is not the business of business to take those decisions. Business, they will argue, has a very clear responsibility to its stakeholders, to optimise productivity and profits. Nevertheless, as part of the social fabric surely we all have a responsibility to the community as a whole. This has become recognised by the movement of companies in their reporting to the so-called "triple bottom-line". It's the traditional bottom line profit of a company, with the added dimensions of social and environmental accountability.

In the political arena, presidents, prime ministers, premiers and ministers are perceived to wield considerable power, and they do. What is often not appreciated, however, is who wields the influence. In many respects, this is even more of an aphrodisiac. How seductive to be able to whisper in the appropriate ear (whether on the pillow or not) and influence the decision.

Powerful people, especially politicians, usually have advisers. Sometimes these advisers do not even have official titles, or have titles that belie their influence. But as every effective lobbyist knows, these are the people you must get to if you hope to get a favourable decision. Yet, I often find that people want to get straight to the minister or the leader, because they are the ones who have the power to take the decision you want taken. Oftentimes they do not have sufficient knowledge or understanding of the issue until their advisers brief them.

Whilst Nietzsche believed that there is a universal need to exercise some kind of power, and I think he is probably right, if you have a choice between the two, choose influence. It usually wins out in the long run. It shapes ideas and creates visions. It is the seed that produces the harvest. As Ruskin said, "Of all the pulpits from which human voice is ever sent forth, there is none from which it reaches so far as from the grave."

Leadership is the exercise of influence based on power. Power is the potential to influence. It is the means not the end. It is essential for leaders to understand the nature of power if they hope to exercise it effectively. Harry Truman understood the difference. He was sympathetic to the problems Eisenhower would face as president. "He'll sit here," Truman said, "and he'll say, 'Do this! Do that!' And nothing will happen. Poor Ike—it won't be a bit like the Army. He'll find it very frustrating."

## Types of Power

French and Raven's (Hughes et al, 1993) taxonomy (1959) has stood the test of time. There have been others developed, but they all have considerable overlap with French and Raven, who identified five different types of power:

1.  *Expert Power*—this is based on the power of knowledge. The possession of specialised knowledge that others might not have puts a person in a position to be able to influence those who do not have that knowledge. It should be recognised, however, by leaders that in perhaps most situations followers will have far greater knowledge than they have in a whole range of areas. In some situations, therefore, followers may exert more power than the leader.

2.  *Referent Power*—refers to the power one has due the strength of the relationship between the leader and the followers. Most of us have role models of different kinds whom we admire, and these role models have a referent power in that we are generally prepared to do what they want us to do. Referent power works both ways in that the relationship also gives the follower significant influence over the leader. In business I had a role model of good behaviour in Sir Roderick Proctor, who was a true gentleman. He was of quiet but firm demeanor, a tall man of military bearing (he had in fact risen from Private to Major during the Second World War), very kind and considerate, very intelligent (a chartered accountant), and a man of the highest integrity. He was chairman of two companies of which I was the CEO.

.   Another rather better known example of the importance of a role model is the relationship between Dwight Eisenhower when he was transferred to Panama at his request to work under General Fox Connor, whom he admired. As Eisenhower later wrote about Connor, "Life with General Connor was a sort of graduate school in military affairs and the humanities, leavened by a man who was experienced in his knowledge of men and their conduct. I can never adequately express my gratitude to this one gentleman...In a lifetime of association with great and good men, he is the one more or less invisible figure to whom I owe an incalculable debt." (Zaleznik, 1992)

3.  *Legitimate Power*—depends on a person's organisational role. This is a seductive source of power, because it depends on formal or official authority. The Pope, a president or prime minister, a general, a CEO of a large company, a platoon sergeant, a factory foreman, a team captain, all hold and exercise legitimate power. However, legitimate authority and leadership are not the same thing. Just because you are captain of the football team does not necessarily make you THE leader or even A leader.     One aspect that has become very relevant in recent years is the control over information. Organisational position can give access to and control of information. In a knowledge economy this can be a very important source of power. In the same way ecological control can be a source of power.

4.  *Reward Power*—is the potential to influence others due to one's control over desired resources. These might be physical or financial resources, salary increases, promotions, bonuses, awards and so on. A cautionary note here in that overemphasis on awards can be negative.

5.    *Coercive Power*—is the opposite of reward power. This refers to the power to punish in a variety of ways. For example, demotion, no bonuses, dismissal, relegation, refusal of resources and so on. An apocryphal story is the comment by Lyndon Johnson, when he was president, to the White House staff that it (the White House) comprised elephants and ants, and he was the only elephant. The message is quite clear.

I would add another type of power to the list. That is *Reputational Power*. Oftentimes the perception of power is just as powerful as actual exercise of the power. If one builds a strong reputation on say the basis of expert knowledge, that reputation will carry on much longer than the expert knowledge may. From the 1960's through the 1990's I was very involved in and prominent in the computer (later information technology) industry. Both my Order of the British Empire in 1982 and my Order of Australia in 1991 were "for service to information technology". My adult children, all fairly computer literate, and my grandchildren go into paroxysms of mirth when they read of me being described as "one of Australia's leading IT practitioners", because they know from my frequent cries for help on my PC or laptop that my expert knowledge at that level leaves much to be desired.

Some years ago on a plane trip, I pulled out a copy of "Windows for Dummies" to read. A couple of days later there was a comment on the front page of the *Sydney Morning Herald*, "Was this the same Ashley Goldsworthy who was President of the Australian Computer Society?" Apparently the person sitting next to me had recognised me, noted what I was reading, and thought it worthy of reporting to the media. All driven, presumably, by that person's knowledge of my reputation.

## Wielding Power

The use of power entails risk. Leaders revel in risk-taking and this is one reason why leaders like to use power.

Perhaps William James' theory of the "once-born" and "twice-born", and his belief that leaders tend to be twice-born personalities, also supports the notion that leaders are more likely to take risks. They are used to struggling and see risk-taking as a way to overcome the obstacles in life.

With respect to the use of power, some generalisations can be made. For example, effective leaders typically take advantage of all their sources of power. Leaders vary according to the extent to which they share power with their followers. Leaders in well-functioning organisations have strong influence over their followers and are also open to being influenced by them.

The exercise of power creates a myriad of relationships in an organisation. Leaders need to be sensitive to these, as they will reinforce or undermine the leader's efforts. In most organisations some people have closer relationships with the leader than others. Those closest to the leader are often referred to as the "in group". Every leader has them. We often hear of "kitchen cabinets" in politics. "Executive Committees" fulfill the same role in business. Quite often they are very small in number. There is a high degree of loyalty, trust and commitment to the leader by the in-group. The leader normally reciprocates this.

Leaders use primarily referent, expert, and reward power to influence followers in the in-group. Typically, leaders use reward, legitimate, and coercive power to influence the out-group. As would be expected, leaders have considerably more influence with the in-group than they have with the out-group. There are, as usual, numerous complexities that impinge upon this oversimplified explanation. The membership of the groups may constantly change, there are different groups for different situations, leaders and followers may have different perceptions of who belongs to which group, what the relationships between members of the groups are, and so on.

Another aspect leaders need to be wary of is the existence of "informal" leaders as opposed to those seen as "formal" leaders. Informal leaders may have more influence than formal leaders and hence need to be treated accordingly.

Wielding power in business has changed significantly over the past decade. Democracy has edged out autocracy in many organisations. The military (and the Catholic Church) remain the exception, although there are many more constraints on leaders in the military than there used to be. There is now much more a "choosing to follow" rather than a "right to lead". Inspirational leadership, therefore, becomes more important. Emotional appeals loom larger than logic. Loyalty supersedes compliance.

An interesting question is, How much power should leaders have? A question that can only be answered by relating to the leader, the followers, and the situation. However, it is worth remembering that power corrupts and absolute power corrupts absolutely.

## Influence

The exercise of influence has been the subject of study for centuries. Aristotle recognised that to persuade required a mix of approaches: the logical (logos), the trust (ethos), and the emotional (pathos).

Leaders recognise the inherent truth in this observation. There must be a connection between the leader and the follower so that the follower identifies with the message of the leader. Leaders have power, but followers have power as well. Influence can be exerted up, down and laterally. Power is the capacity to exert influence , but how is influence exerted?

Logical persuasion is an obvious tactic. The use of factual evidence and rational persuasion are useful tools. Inspirational appeals designed to arouse emotions and enthusiasm often work. People like to be consulted, and this can encourage participation. Personal appeals from the leader to the followers are often effective, especially if the leader has strong referent power. Appealing to followers as friends, colleagues, and so on will often bring results.

Ingratiation is a technique that is sometimes useful. If followers feel kindly disposed towards the leader, if they are satisfied rather than dissatisfied, they are more likely to respond positively to a request. If the situation is appropriate, the exchange of favours might achieve the desired result.

It can be useful to use the support of others to influence the target. A coalition is often more persuasive than a single person. One technique that everybody is familiar with is using threats and pressure to achieve the desired response. And finally, the leader can resort to legitimising tactics using the power of office to achieve the outcome sought.

Perhaps a sense of humour is a useful ingredient, as Willie Sutton, the notorious bank robber in the United States, once said, "A gun and a smile are more effective than a smile by itself."

Having exercised influence, the challenge remains of achieving the desired outcome. This is not always the case. What leaders hope to achieve from followers is commitment ; the willingness of followers to go to whatever length is necessary to carry out the request from the leader.

What they may get, however, is compliance, where the followers are willing to do what is asked but no more. They are not enthusiastic, but rather apathetic and will only make a minimal effort. They will not go the extra mile. The problem is that the leader has influenced behaviour, but not attitudes. The followers are not convinced that the decision or action is the best thing to do, or even that it will be effective in accomplishing the desired purpose. This is a dangerous outcome for the leader, because he may not realise this is the outcome and be misled into a sense of false security.

The least desirable outcome is, of course, resistance. The followers rebel and refuse to do the leader's bidding. Resistance can be exercised in a number of ways other than straight out refusal. Followers may make excuses why the request cannot be carried out. They may try to persuade the leader to change the request. They may appeal to higher authorities to override the instruction. They may delay, hoping the issue or the leader will go away. They may make a pretence of complying, but sabotage the task. In these ways, subtle resistance can be difficult to detect and leaders need to be continually sensitive to these possibilities.

Research has indicated that the most effective tactics are inspirational appeals and consultation. The effectiveness of rational persuasion depends very much on how it is used. Ingratiation and exchanging favours can be effective in influencing followers and peers, but seldom effective in influencing superiors.

Not surprisingly, the least effective tactics for influencing followers are exerting pressure, coalition, and legitimating tactics. These tactics are unlikely to result in commitment, but may elicit compliance, especially when combined with rational persuasion.

# CHAPTER 5 -

# Communication

*Admitting you're wrong is easy; knowing you're wrong is difficult.*

Effective communication is the lynchpin in the leadership process. In many respects leadership is all about communication. Leaders have to be confident that their followers are in no doubt as to what is required of them.

Communication can be in a variety of forms: oral, visual, behavioural, sound, touch, smell, written, electronic, or a combination of all. Communication is a two-way process. It involves listening and understanding. The more open and transparent the process is the better. In the leadership process, face-to-face communication is usually more effective than remote communication by telephone, television, e-mail, letter, or personal emissaries. The latter forms may be more effective for communicating detailed information, but inspiring and motivating is helped by personal and direct contact.

One of the frequent comments on why Pope John Paul II had been so successful as a communicator was that he had met more people in person than anyone else in history, even though those meetings may have been in huge groups of people. Part of the current mantra is that people turned up to "see" Pope John Paul II, but they turn up to "hear" Pope Benedict XVI.

Face-to-face communication exposes much more of the individual. Two-way exchanges require reactions in seconds or even fractions of a second. The general tone and direction of the discussion depends on both people. Leadership aspects become much more apparent than in reading a letter.

Communication networks are important in helping to ensure messages reach all concerned. Electronic networks provide the ultimate in speed and coverage of the targeted audience.

Communication networks are what I call the spider-web (no pun on the world wide web) of the organisation. The most effective organisations are those where communications are unfettered ; where information flows are dictated by need, not by structure, person or process. You only need to touch a spider's web at any point and the spider immediately becomes aware of the contact. The information flow is immediate.

For example, the trapdoor spider hides in a tunnel that can be closed with a door. If the prey walks over a signal thread, the door is opened and the spider grabs it. That's effective communication.

Communication patterns within groups are both formal and informal. Leaders need to utilise both. When you think about it, almost every aspect of leadership depends on communication.

## Articulating a Vision

Communication is about articulating the vision in a way that everybody understands and is inspired by. It requires constant reinforcement. It has to be repeated at every opportunity. The message has to be consistent and it has to touch the heart as well as the mind.

Jack Welch, Chairman and CEO of General Electric from 1981 to 2001, is regarded as one of the most successful CEOs in America. Welch repeats himself purposely. "In leadership you have to exaggerate every statement you make. You've got to repeat it a thousand times…. Over-statements are needed to move large organisations." Welch understood the need for, and the value of, linking messages to a benefit. He asked people to cut travel costs by 30%. He wrapped the message in the context of integrating work and life. He pointed out that his directive would give managers 30% more time with their families.

Many people are passionate about an idea, a project, or a business. What distinguishes a leader is their ability to communicate that passion in a way which makes other people want to go with them. When a strategy is developed, it has to be communicated to everyone involved.

Ray Kroc's sense of enthusiasm for McDonald's and the hamburger was legendary. He created the quick service restaurant, as we know it, by sheer force of will and salesmanship. He became so excited about what he sold that he persuaded others to follow. Kroc, however, was more than a salesman. He was a leader. If not, he never could have built a company. As a result, he built an organisation of people who could do things Kroc could not. Initially, the force of his personality and the logic of his vision for building a restaurant system based upon standardisation of quality, convenience, and service, however, drew franchisees and employees, to Kroc. Employees, franchisees, and vendors alike shared in Kroc's vision of the future.

One of the main reasons CEOs fail is not lack of vision, poor strategy, or wrong products, but lack of execution brought on by failure of communication. Some years ago, (1999) *Fortune* magazine explored why corporations fail. Of the ten reasons cited, four were a failure of communication. Effective leadership is effective communications.

## Values

Communication is not just about the message. Leaders have to sell themselves as people, with certain beliefs and values. Followers are not persuaded only by words or actions, they need to see trust, integrity, and honesty in their leaders. They also have to be convinced of the sincerity of their leaders and their leaders' belief in the message they are trying to sell.

The sexual abuse scandal that has swept through the Catholic Church is a sad example of what can happen when the values of an organisation do not match the actions of its leaders. The actions of many bishops in refusing to believe pedophilia allegations in the first place and then compounding their mistake by transferring priests rather than taking disciplinary action was a sad dereliction of leadership responsibility.

## The Arts

One critical aspect of communication often overlooked is the art of listening. I well remember the political leader who suffered an unexpected election defeat and was urged by his organisation to visit community and business leaders, and listen to what they had to say.

After a number of such visits, the organisation started to receive some negative feedback. When confronted, the leader maintained that he had been doing as asked. He said he had spent hours explaining the party's policies and his intentions to business leaders. This was precisely the problem. He did not understand that listening was a critical part of the art of leadership. He was deposed as a leader soon thereafter.

The art of persuasion is one of the most valuable tools of a leader. "Leadership is leaders inducing followers to act for certain goals that present *the values* and the motivations—the wants and needs, the aspirations and expectations—of both leaders and followers," wrote James MacGregor Burns in *Leadership,* a seminal study of the topic.

Just as one can learn about leadership, one can hone communication skills. Some of the great communicators spent their lives honing their skills. Churchill was sixty-five at the outbreak of World War II. Ronald Reagan, known as the Great Communicator, was president for most of his seventies. Both men dedicated their lives to developing the skills of communication.

Mintzberg (1989) captures the central importance of communication when he describes the various "roles" of those in charge of organisations. First, there are the interpersonal roles of being a figurehead of the organisation, a leader, and as a liaison person. All these roles require communication skills. Then there are informational roles. These comprise being the nerve centre of the organisation, a disseminator of ideas and directions, a monitor, and a spokesman. All of these require communication.

Finally, there are decisional roles as an entrepreneur, a disturbance handler, a resource allocator, and a negotiator. All of these roles require communication skills. This analysis neatly highlights the centrality and importance of communication in the leadership process. Leaders are about making a difference. They are trying to motivate people to come on the journey with them. Their communications have to identify these differences. They may be both metaphorical and literal.

## Simplicity

Politics gives many good examples of the effectiveness of simplicity and repetition in communicating a message. Bill Clinton's first presidential election campaign adopted the slogan "It's the Economy, Stupid" to remind everyone on the staff what the real issue was and it worked. In Australia, the

"It's Time" slogan of the Labor Party swept Gough Whitlam into office as Prime Minister in 1972.

In May 1986, Paul Keating was dealing with what, until then, was Australia's worst current account deficit on record. He said on radio, "We must let Australians know truthfully, honestly, earnestly, just what sort of an international hole Australia is in." The cause, according to Treasurer Keating, was the Australian dollar, uncomfortably high at 71.24 US cents. But two words during an interview with John Laws sent the Australian dollar and financial markets into a tailspin. Keating said, "The only thing to do is to slow the growth down to a canter, and once that happens, once you slow the growth under three per cent, unemployment starts to rise again… Well, then you're gone, you know, you're a banana republic." The Australian dollar fell 10 percent in the days and weeks after the banana republic comment.

Another well-known slogan was the "Fightback" campaign of John Hewson, then Leader of the Opposition . Hewson was determined to make a break with what he saw as the weak pragmatism of past Liberal leaders. In November 1991, he launched "Fightback," a radical economic policy package. The key elements of the package were an introduction of a consumption tax, called the goods and services tax (GST); the compensatory abolition of a range of other taxes, such as sales tax; deep cuts in income tax for the middle and upper-middle classes; and increases in pensions and benefits to compensate the poor for the rise in prices flowing from the GST.

The package was at first well-received, and was welcomed as an idealistic alternative to the rather cynical pragmatism which had come to mark the Hawke government. Hawke and his Treasurer, John Kerin, were unable to mount an effective response and in December 1991, Keating successfully challenged Hawke and became Prime Minister.

Through 1992 Keating mounted a ruthless scare campaign against the Fightback package, and particularly against the GST, which he described as an attack on the working class in that it shifted the tax burden from direct taxation of the wealthy to indirect taxation of the mass of consumers. Keating famously described Hewson (a former Professor of Economics) as a "feral abacus."

The complications of the new package were famously demonstrated in the "Birthday Cake Interview", in which Hewson was unable to answer a question posed by journalist Michael Willessee about whether or not a birthday cake would cost more or less under a Coalition government. Hewson was instead forced into a series of circumlocutions about whether the cake would be decorated, have ice cream in it and so on.

Keating's campaign was demagogic and in some ways unfair, but Hewson's personal detestation of Keating clouded his judgement, and he lacked the political skills to counter Keating effectively. At the March 1993 election, Keating defeated Hewson in what many had described as "the unloseable election". (As Federal President of the Liberal Party during that campaign I also paid the price and lost the Presidency later that year.)

In business, and in many other spheres as well, the adage of KISS "Keep It Simple, Stupid" is very apt advice when applied to communication. Leaders need to understand that to communicate effectively they need to "connect" with the audience. Reason and rationality may be the answer for some, but by far the most important is emotional connection. It's the hearts not the minds that the leader has to capture. Logic will not get you to leap out of the trench, but emotion might. Great communication, as evidenced by great communicators like Churchill and Martin Luther King, is based on emotion as well as reason. Whilst the message may be consistent, the language, the content, the mode of delivery, even the timing, has to be targeted to the specific audience. A new product launch to senior executives will be quite different from that to front-line salespeople.

## **Building Bridges**

Leaders have to build bridges to their audience. They have to get on the same wave-length. The audience has to feel their emotional commitment. Audiences often forget *what* has been said, but they can always recall *how* it was said. One of the best examples of this is Adolf Hitler. At his rallies he spoke with almost hypnotic persuasion. There are many accounts by people who were at these rallies who did not remember much of what Hitler said, but had vivid and lasting impressions of how he said it. Hitler built very effective bridges to his audience. In his speeches he played to the feelings of the German people at that time. He told them what they felt, what they thought, what they wanted. He became the personification of the aspirations of the German people.

However, being an effective communicator does not necessarily mean being a great orator. In fact, few leaders are great orators, but many are great communicators. As Winston Churchill said, "Of all the talents bestowed upon men, none is so precious as the gift of oratory."

In contrast, we have Mohandas 'Mahatma" Gandhi. He was not an orator, few even heard, let alone remembered, his words. His communication technique was leading by example, not words. He may not have been a great orator, but he was a great communicator. He understood the power of symbols. Imagine Gandhi in a three-piece suit rather than a loincloth (which revolted Churchill).

John F. Kennedy visited Berlin in June 1963, and a wall divided the city, East from West. Who will forget his connecting with the audience by breaking into German: "Today, in the world of freedom, the proudest boast is: *Ich bin ein Berliner.*" Or his inaugural address: "Ask not what your country can do for you. Ask what you can do for your country."

Jimmy Carter was an effective bridge builder. Largely unknown before his election in 1976, in his campaign he would begin along these lines. "I'm Jimmy Carter. I come from a small town in the south. I'm a farmer, a churchgoer, and a family man. I live with my wife, Rosalynn, and my young daughter, Amy. I served in the navy and I was a nuclear engineer. I was governor of Georgia." Carter connected with a large part of any audience. He had built a bridge. They could relate to him.

Rudy Giuliani was the mayor of New York at the time of the attack on the World Trade Center. He played a major role in the days and weeks following that attack. He, in fact, became a national hero because of his leadership in those trying times. Giuliani, in his book *Leadership,* emphasises the importance of communications. He was insistent about getting the media involved. He gave almost constant on-the-spot interviews. Giuliani demonstrates an instinctive understanding of the fact that leaders only achieve through the efforts of others. His book is filled with the names of people he encountered on that fateful day.

An important aspect of connecting with the audience, especially in a business, is to make everybody feel they are an important part of the organisation. Winston Churchill had a great talent for this. He made individual Britons feel they were on centre stage. His wartime radio broadcasts made them feel important. He convinced them that their individual contributions were an essential part of winning the war.

Mother Teresa was a powerful storyteller. She was famous for telling stories of the people to whom she ministered.

## Famous Styles

Leaders can learn a lot about effective communication by studying the techniques and styles of famous communicators and heeding their lessons. For example, Churchill's love of short words. This makes for simplicity with eloquence. Other famous communicators, such as Ralph Waldo Emerson, Abraham Lincoln (his Gettysburg Address), and Franklin D. Roosevelt ("Be sincere, be brief, be seated") are full of lessons.

Other techniques, such as figures of speech and so on, can add enormously to the impact of the message. Metaphors such as Churchill's "blood, toil, sweat and tears"; Paul Keating's "banana republic"; Bill Hayden's "drover's dog"; Martin Luther King's "I Have a Dream" speech, are examples that have entered the lexicon. Claude Levi-Strauss, the French social anthropologist, wrote that "metaphor, far from being a decoration that is added to language, purifies it and restores it to its original nature."

Mother Theresa communicated through her prayers, writing, and public appearances. George C. Marshall, speaking to the U.S. Congress on the need for military preparedness, mobilised the armed forces to defeat fascism and later to rebuild a broken Europe.

One of the greatest communicators we have seen in our time was Pope John Paul II. He was a charismatic communicator who managed to get his messages across not only to Catholics, but to peoples of all religions, not just by his words, but by his deeds, his personality, his compassion, his moral stature, and his obvious love and generosity to all. There was no doubt as to the values that John Paul believed in. His messages were crystal clear and those who disagreed with him did not dissuade him, and there were many. There was no doubt in anyone's mind that he was totally committed to what he believed and that was reflected in his communications, be they public speeches, papal encyclicals, or personal audiences.

Any discussion on effective communication would be incomplete if Jesus Christ was not mentioned. His whole life was one of communication. The great storyteller. After two thousand years we still remember His stories, His parables. Anecdote and storytelling are powerful forms of communication. In business they are also a very useful way of maintaining corporate memory.

Another outstanding example of communication is Muhammad (peace be upon him), the founder of Islam. For 22 years, Muhammad received revelations from the Archangel Gabriel. These revelations became the Qur'an. It is reputedly (I do not read Arabic) an outstanding example of Arabic prose and poetry, and to be perfect in its grammar. But Muhammad was illiterate. Muhammad's followers wrote down the Qur'an on whatever was at hand. It is the "standing miracle" at the centre of the Islamic faith.

## Credibility

A leader's credibility rests heavily on communications. Leaders need to build trust with their followers, and trust depends very much on what is communicated and how it is communicated. Credibility is a leader's currency. This means there can be no equivocation, no dishonesty, no ambivalence, no insincerity, no misrepresentation, and no cock-and-bull. On the other hand, do not be frightened to admit mistakes. Leaders who acknowledge their errors or misjudgements hearten followers. Bill Clinton acknowledged his misdeeds, but it was too late. His credibility was destroyed.

One thing I have always practised is to tell the bad news first. People then come to realise that they do not have to lie awake at night wondering what might be going on. They can relax in the knowledge that they will always know the bad news and therefore, do not have to worry. This helps greatly in building trust and confidence in people. It is particularly useful in building trust between a CEO and a Board of Directors. If the Board knows the CEO will always tell them the bad news up front, it goes a long way to establishing their trust in him. Communicating up is just as important as communicating down and across.

It has been reported (*The Weekend Australian*, 24-25 January 2009) that John Thain, head of the Bank of America's global banking and wealth management operations lost his job because he lost the confidence of his CEO, when the CEO heard of mounting losses from a transition team handling the business rather than from Thain himself. Always tell the boss the bad news first, and be the first to tell him.

Colin Powell said that if a leader is not hearing bad news, something is wrong. "The day soldiers stop bringing you their problems is the day you stopped leading them. They have either lost confidence that you can help them or concluded that you do not care. Either case is a failure of leadership."

The *Challenger* disaster is another example. The engineers at Morton-Thiokol knew that the O-rings in the booster rockets were not certified to withstand freezing temperatures. Yet when NASA pushed for a launch in near-freezing weather, the engineers had no ready way to communicate their knowledge. The "no bad news" culture that permeated the space program at that time thwarted open dialogue between the supplier's engineers and program leadership. All the engineers could do at launch time was watch with helpless agony as the Challenger's booster exploded in midair.

Jack Welch said that a CEO's greatest failing was "being the last to know". The long-time chairman of one of Australia's major banks was recently (Dec. 2008) reported as saying the first he knew of a major financial debacle involving the bank was when he read about it in the newspaper. Welch made a point of surrounding himself with people who would give it to him straight. He said that a leader who never hears bad news is hopelessly out of touch. In business, but in many other spheres as well, it is important not to over-promise. Only promise what you can deliver, and deliver what you promise. Above all, do what you say you will do.

As I so often emphasise, leadership is all about people. People communicate, and communication is the glue that holds an organisation together. It is the way that people relate to one another. Effective communications at all levels must become a core competency of every organisation. And leaders play a special role, because their communications have to be understood by everybody.

Leaders need to appreciate that their messages must be about the big issues that reflect the present and future of the organisation. They must be sensitive to the fact that their messages reflect the vision, mission, and culture of the organisation. In doing so, there must be a consistency in communications which exemplify stated values and behaviour. And no message can be effectively communicated unless it is done so with persistent regularity and frequency.

One thing all these leaders have in common is commitment to a cause or goal larger than themselves. As such, leaders need to integrate communications into everything they do as leaders. No leader will ever achieve his or her goal without being an effective communicator.

# CHAPTER 6 -

# Motivation

*Struggling uphill is far better than sliding downhill.*

## Values

Part of the secret of good leadership is the alignment of values with goals. Everybody has values and they are a critical element in a person's make-up. If a person is given a goal which in some way conflicts with their value set, then they will face a very difficult situation. Leadership is about resolving, not creating conflict.

If a person has pride in delivering a quality output and puts their effort into always trying to deliver the highest quality in whatever they do, to ask them to do otherwise is likely to fail. It will be intensely demotivating. For example, someone who is responsible for training apprentices and treasures the quality of the graduates they produce is judged on the number of trainees who successfully complete the course. On the one hand, their performance is being judged on numbers being put through, but their own sense of values is telling them that the quality of the graduates is more important. But to satisfy their preferred outcome may well jeopardise the rewards the system will give them.

What will they do? The effective leader will be sensitive to these sorts of issues and will take them into account when setting goals and objectives which are designed to motivate people.

## Setting Goals

This issue of setting goals to motivate people is an interesting challenge. By far the most common manner of setting goals is to quantify them. The underlying philosophy is if it cannot be quantified, it cannot be measured. But leadership is all about people and management is all about numbers. People are motivated by intangibles, such as values, ideas, competition and commitment. People are more excited by the challenge to build a car of high quality (a value) than they are to build one of low cost (a number). It is much easier (and far more effective for the business) to enthuse bank tellers to build friendly relationships with customers than it is to ask them to serve a specified number per day.

Leaders have to tap into the internal drivers of people. Values such as personal excellence, pride in a job well done, and the respect of colleagues, are very powerful motivating forces and often underestimated in the response they will engender.

When it comes to setting goals, I am a fervent supporter of setting goals that require that bit of extra stretch to achieve them. And not just a little bit of stretch, but a lot. Challenging goals usually create strong motivation. Collins and Porras have described this practice of highly visionary companies adopting bold missions as BHAGS (Big Hairy Audacious Goals). They believe they are powerful mechanisms in stimulating progress. A good example on a somewhat larger scale is Kennedy's commitment in 1961 to put a man on the moon. That really was a BHAG. And it was a goal that had, in most people's minds, little chance of being achieved.

A BHAG can serve as a powerful unifying force. It can create immense team spirit. One of the beauties of BHAGS, such as putting a man on the moon, is that they are unambiguous. They do not need a committee to define them. And it is also very clear when the goal has been achieved. Everybody in the team is under no illusion as to what has to be achieved. Moreover, it is a simple goal. It does not have to be expanded. It can be easily grasped. It does not need a carefully worded Mission Statement.

GE's goal of being Number 1 or Number 2 in every market they served had similar benefits. Nobody in GE was under any misapprehension of what was required. It was clear, compelling and challenging. It got the juices flowing. Leaders are audacious and BHAGS sit very neatly with their belief in being able to achieve beyond the norm. They want to work outside the comfort zone.

At the turn of the 19th century, Theodore Roosevelt said, "Far better to dare mighty things, to win glorious triumphs, even though checkered by failure, than to take rank with those poor spirits who neither enjoy much nor suffer much, because they live in the gray twilight that knows not victory, nor defeat."

## A Lonely Job

In the early days of a career, relationships are developed with peers, which oftentimes grow into friendships. As people progress through their careers, they tend to move from roles that are primarily management to roles that offer more opportunities for leadership. It is inevitable that this will affect relationships.

Many people who would be leaders think that close relationships with colleagues will help in their leadership role. They will not. They will cause more angst, hurt and disappointment than they are worth. Even worse, they may seduce the leader into making decisions that are unreasonably influenced by the relationship. In other words, making the wrong decision.

Motivation is not about developing relationships with followers, other than those which reinforce the desired outcome. Intimacy and friendship is not necessary, or even desirable, for effectiveness.

Long experience has convinced me that leadership at senior levels works better if leaders keep some distance between themselves and their followers. After all, it does impose an intolerable burden to sack a senior executive who happens to be your tennis partner and regularly comes to dinner at your house with his wife. For these reasons, introverts often find it much easier to move up the hierarchy. Whilst as a young manager the extrovert will have many friends and will be the life of the office party, moving up the hierarchy into more responsible positions will make it much harder to handle increasing power and at the same time sustain friendships. Leadership can be a lonely process and if that is a problem, do something else.

## Fear and Love

Fear and love (deep affection) are the extremes of the emotional spectrum available to leaders to motivate their followers. It takes a rare individual to engender love to the extent of it being the motivation for followers.

Great religious leaders (Jesus Christ, Mohammed) undoubtedly engender love. Great political leaders (Mahatma Gandhi, John Kennedy) can sometimes arouse deep emotions in their followers. I have no doubt there are times when military leaders engender such emotions. General Monash had such a reputation. It is unusual for business leaders to tap into such deep emotional wells. Business leaders are more likely to be admired, respected, or well liked rather than loved.

It is a typical bell curve: fear and love on the extremes and the centre filled with admiration, respect, friendship, loyalty and devotion. Fear is an emotion that is central to leadership, but not often admitted as such. Hitler and Stalin are just two recent examples of leaders who ruled largely by fear.

There is no doubt that the fear of failure can be a most motivating force. Fear is a powerful human emotion and leaders who ignore it as part of their armoury deprive themselves of a really useful weapon.

What you need to do is recognise the appropriate way to use fear. I have worked for CEOs (you never work <u>with</u> these CEOs) that used fear as their only management tool. I have seen grown men come out of their offices humiliated and embarrassed to the stage of tears. Such people are invariably bullies and if you stand up to them from day one, you have some chance of coming out on top. In many cases, however, they will endure.

Michael Knight, the Minister for the Olympics in Sydney in 2000, is reported (*The Australian*, 5/10/00, p. 13) to have said, "It doesn't matter if they hate me, as long as they fear me." He had a reputation that matched that philosophy and after some trenchant criticism of him for some particularly petty and mean-spirited decisions, resigned from politics in the week following the Games—missed by few. This is what I call mal-fear, "bad" fear and is to be avoided. Such people are to be despised and should be treated with contempt.

A very common fear is fear of change. This fear can be used to stifle change. Management is too often conducive to risk averse strategies. It is not in the nature of management to seek change.

Leadership is all about initiating change and discarding the status quo. To do this it is often much easier to create a crisis than it is to create a vision so appealing that everyone is immediately supportive and committed. Therefore, leadership has to replace the fear of change with the fear of losing, of falling behind, of seeing your competitors charge ahead because they have embraced change and you have not. This is fear that is a positive fear. It not only welcomes change; it positively seeks it out for the ultimate benefit of the group. This is a fear that thrives on change. This is the sort of fear that effective leaders use to their advantage. This is what I call bon-fear, "good" fear.

Nevertheless, you need to be careful that in some situations even "good" fear has the potential for negative results. A study done by Hindle at Swinburne University (*The Australian Financial Review*, 6/10/00) reported that fear of failure was enough to deter 36 percent of Australian adults from embarking on entrepreneurial ventures. Hindle said, "This is a potentially alarming finding. Fear of failure is a good differentiator between countries. In the United States failure is seen as part of the rite of passage towards success." He said that if Australia was able to change the stigma of fear of failure through education, it would have major implications for the future of the country and its ability to generate successful, job-creating businesses.

The absence of fear can also be a strong motivating culture. Masaru Ibuka, the Founder of the Sony Corporation, said, "We worked furiously (to realise our goals). Because we didn't have fear, we could do something drastic."

## Adding Value

One of the differences in leadership at senior levels is that you are dealing with executives who have leadership responsibilities themselves; in large organisations they may be very substantial responsibilities. What you have to do in those circumstances is add value to what they are already doing. This brings out the coaching role of the leader.

At this level, experience is a must. Leaders must earn the respect of their executives and they will only do this by performance. It is important for leaders to remember that their role is that—a leader. They are not there as the chief expert in every or any aspect of the business. All of the senior executives will (should) know more about their part of the business than they do. They are there because they can bring a clear vision as to where they are heading, they can communicate that in a way which enthuses and motivates them, and they can articulate a strategy to achieve that vision.

Survey after survey brings home the point that money is not the prime motivator in driving performance, although the salaries being paid to some CEOs in recent times certainly bring this into question. In instances where quite obscene amounts of tens of millions of dollars are paid to CEOs despite poor performance of the company, one has to question the responsibility of the Boards of Directors and the effect such payments do have on the rest of the organisation.

Leaders certainly should be strongly motivated to work for reasons other than money or status. Part of the secret of motivating others is the very clear message that what is driving you is something beyond personal rewards. The drive to be the best, or to be first, or to be the most efficient, or to be the least expensive (rather nicer than being the cheapest), are the sorts of drivers that enable you to build emotional fervour.

Adding value to individuals is a strong motivating force. People respond to being recognised and appreciate the interest taken in their own development. Good staff will pursue their own development, but even then they appreciate the advice and support of leaders as to what they should do to enhance their careers.

## **Rewarding Effort**

There is an old saying that you can lead a horse to water, but you cannot make it drink. People are no different. They will only do what they want to do or are motivated to do.

Contrary to common opinion, money is not the most effective way to motivate people. Extensive research over the years has repeatedly confirmed this and my own experience supports it. People certainly appreciate monetary rewards, but there does come a time when it recedes into the background as a strong incentivator. Other factors, such as positive reinforcement, satisfying employee needs, giving greater challenges, restructuring jobs, and celebrating successes are more motivating.

One aspect of rewards which I have always insisted upon is transparency. Whatever goals people are set and however their performance is going to be measured, it should be perfectly clear to them at the outset how it is going to work.

Wherever possible there should be minimum, and preferably none, discretionary judgements by the leader or anyone else. If peoples' rewards are subject to some sort of value judgement by others, they lose a lot of their motivating force. There are some aspects of performance which may rightly (perhaps only) be done by subjective judgement. Aspects such as attitude, responsiveness, and team spirit, are going to have to be value judgements. But wherever possible the person should know how they are performing and what their reward is at that point in time. Why is this important?

Firstly, because motivation is a constant not a periodic stimulus. Therefore, a person must be able to gauge at any time how they are performing against their goals. They cannot do this if the measure is subject to someone's discretionary judgement.

Secondly, goals normally extend over a period of time and achievement is normally progressive through that period. It is important, therefore, that motivation is constant and this is reinforced by a knowledge of performance.

## **Inspiration**

Leadership is about inspiring people. Inspiring them not only to perform, but to excel themselves. Inspiration is often equated to charisma. Charismatic leaders can certainly inspire, but there are very few truly charismatic leaders. How then do the rest of aspiring leaders inspire?

The best advice I can give is "be yourself". This was the advice that Jack Welch gave when asked by *Fortune* magazine what the best advice he had ever received was. When the *Harvard Business Review* published its first special themed issue in December 2001, the topic was "Breakthrough Leadership: It's Personal". To inspire people, a leader, above all, has to be credible. Leadership is about relationships, and people will eventually see through a facade of falsity. This means that a leader has to be authentic. I have emphasised elsewhere the importance of integrity. Integrity is critical to credibility and authenticity.

Successful leaders recognise those aspects of their personalities which attract followers to them and leverage those characteristics for major effect. This is not only legitimate ; it is sensible.

As I have said, leadership is a process not a position, and people want to be led by a person not by a position holder, and that person has to be real, with strengths and weaknesses. Good leaders magnify those personality characteristics to which followers respond and they may well be weaknesses as well as strengths. However, the weaknesses need to be humanising ones and they need to be attractive, not repelling. People are not inspired by perfection. They can be inspired by human foibles, which often make leaders seem more like themselves.

Inspirational leaders are intuitive. They can sense what works in a particular situation. Sporting coaches are good examples of inspirational leaders and how they manage relationships. They continually have to inspire players on a personal one-to-one basis, but at the same time they have to be brutal in dropping them if they are not performing. And they have to do this week in, week out, while maintaining harmony and morale in the team.

# CHAPTER 7 -

# Those Out in Front

*Never enter a contest you will not be disappointed at losing.*

## Who Are They?

Thomas Edison is credited with saying: "Every significant accomplishment in the history of civilisation was once considered impossible by all but the few, and it is those few who become the leaders."

A person who is a brilliant leader with a particular set of people in a particular situation may turn out to be a hopeless leader when any of those components are changed. Change the people, change the time, change the environment, change any one of a thousand factors and the outcome is likely to be different.

Would Winston Churchill have been such an outstanding leader if World War II had not occurred? Who knows? There is a distinct possibility he would not have. Some would say a distinct probability. What was it that enabled Julius Caesar, Charlemagne, and Alexander the Great to build great empires? How did some rather undistinguished people (Claudius Caesar, Adolph Hitler) rise to positions of great power?

Hardly a day goes by in Australia when you do not read in the media a plea for "leadership". This may be in politics, it may be in business, it may be in religion, it may be in education, and it may be in anything. We must not confuse leaders with famous or well-known people. We are talking about people who change the course of events. They may not be world-shattering events, but they do affect change, they do affect people, and they do involve the achievement of desired outcomes.

In business, most people pass through the stage of management on the way to leadership. It is considerably easier to plan, control, and organise activities rather than initiate change and deal with difficult and intangible people issues. We emphasise the importance of vision in leadership. Hand-in-hand with vision goes four other essential virtues, the Four C's: Courage, Conviction, Compassion, and Commitment. Leaders need to be able to take others with them down the path they want to travel. Leadership is all about developing people. Leaders should be endeavouring to grow others, not themselves. They will have no hope of doing this if they themselves are in any doubt. Self-doubt is a cancer for a leader. If their own self-confidence is destroyed, there is little hope of the followers being enthused.

Leaders need an ego. They need an unshakeable belief in their own judgement, their direction, and the consequences of their own actions. Leadership is not for wimps. This does not mean that leaders have blind faith in everything they do or that they never question their own decisions. Above all else leaders are human, but the difference is they never let self-doubt rule their actions.

When I started work some 50 years ago, the number one job in a company was the Managing Director. Everybody knew the MD and everybody knew he was top dog. In large companies, when you became the MD you knew you had a job until retirement. If the company was big enough (a BHP, a CSR, a Commonwealth Bank), the job also carried a knighthood. After retirement you could look forward to Chairman of the Board of other well-known companies. That has now all changed. The average tenure of CEOs of large companies is between three to seven years. Knighthoods were dispensed with two decades ago. Becoming MD is no longer a job until retirement.

However, the most significant change in the context of this book is the displacement of the title Managing Director by the Chief Executive Officer or CEO. Almost invariably today the title is either Managing Director and Chief Executive Officer, or just Chief Executive Officer. Why is this significant? After all, it is just a change in title. It is much more than that. It is a recognition that the nature of the position should be more concerned with leadership than with management.

When I first became a CEO over 30 years ago (and I have since been CEO of 10 organisations) I was not a member of the board, but carried the title General Manager. When I was approached to take the position, one of my demands was that my title would be General Manager and Chief Executive. I recognised at that time that the key role was that of Chief Executive. That is, there was no doubt in anybody's mind who was responsible for the ultimate decisions, who was responsible, with the support of the board, for the direction of the company. Today that is commonplace for the very same reason. Being a member of the board, and even being the managing director, is not as important in perception and reality as being the Chief Executive.

In the American context this is emphasised even more where either the Chairman or the President (Managing Director) may be Chief Executive Officer. It is the designation of CEO which is the critical one.

I watched an interview with Scott McNealy, the founder of Sun Microsystems, one of the most successful computer suppliers in the world. He was described as "CEO", not Chairman or President, but CEO , because this is seen as the most accurate description of his role and what it means.

Gary Pemberton, former Chairman of NSW Racing,  Chairman of Qantas and Billabong, former CEO of Brambles, and former Non-executive Director of the Commonwealth Bank, CRA, Rio Tinto, CSR, Tabcorp, and Fairfax has said (The Bulletin, 26 April 2005) that when he was offered the top job at Brambles, he told his chairman the deal would be that he (Pemberton) would run the company and the chairman would go to the cocktail parties and the dinners –and that is how it worked.

Pemberton is also reported as saying, "You can get away with a bad chairman, get away with a bad board, provided you've got a good CEO. But you can never get away with an ordinary CEO." When asked whether even the best chair could make up for a good CEO, he said, "Nup. All he can do is get rid of him and get a good one."

Compared with 30 years ago, CEOs today have a different set of priorities. Management is about containment of risk. It is rational, measurable, and it moves minds. Leadership is intuitive, non-measurable, and it moves hearts. To do this leaders must be passionate. It is passion which provides the momentum which drives leaders. Leaders have to be driven in the sense of having an inner energy which propels them towards their goals. Passion allows them to pass on this energy to those they are leading. Managers do not have this passion. Entrepreneurs do, but shepherds do not.

A non-energetic leader is an oxymoron. Leaders not only have to be energetic, they are energetic. This is not a question of working 16-hour days , it is about the burning fire in the belly. Every day you leap out of bed to do something that day to make a difference. Jack Welch says it is, "All about energy, energize, and edge-E cubed I call it. You've got to have incredible energy to lead any organisation. You've got to be on fire, if you will. It's a part of it. You've got to be able to energize people... You can have all the energy in the world, but if you don't get other people energized, nothing happens." (Lowe, p.204)

One issue I do not intend to explore is the different types of leader and leadership discussed in the scholarly literature. Much has been written in recent years of charismatic, transformational, and transactional leaders. There are proponents who argue a fine set of differences between the three. There are critics who argue that it is nothing but another perspective on the difference between leadership and management. Whether or not it is a useful distinction, you can judge for yourself when reading the literature.

The point to remember in a book such as this is what practical benefit flows from debating such a distinction. It may well be useful in better understanding the nature of leadership, but there remains much work to be done to buttress the theory with practical evidence of real companies and real leaders, and real sustained change. In somewhat the same vein, I do not intend to explore the gender issue.

A common misconception is that running an organisation is the same as being a leader. It is not. Being the CEO or the MD does not automatically confer leadership status. This has been further confused in recent years by the terminology changes I discussed above. There tends to be an automatic inference that "chief executive" must mean "leader". If the chief executive is not the leader, then who the hell is? This is a valid question and the answer may be that there is no leader in the organisation or that there are leaders, but they are lower down in the hierarchy.

At times in the life cycle of a company, the purpose of top management is to maintain success. In a large organisation this requires a complex set of skills, it requires careful planning, but it does not require the development of a new vision for the company. That requires a leader. It requires much more than rational decision-making, it requires something more intuitive, more innate, something honed by experience and personality.

Clearly those who bear the title of chief executive, or general, or arch-bishop, hold executive power and authority within their organisations. But authority or power conferred by right of office does not confer leadership. It often does produce what I have called the "shepherd". Someone to main-tain the status quo, to keep things on an even keel, to focus on the needs of the followers, and generally to avoid chaos and risk ; to shepherd the organ-isation through a period of calm progress without dramatic change.

Doug Ivester, a Chairman and CEO of Coca-Cola, is a good example. Ivester was a brilliant manager who for ten years had impressed CEO Roberto Goizueta with his hard work and creative execution of company strategy. But the Board pushed out Ivester, after only two years in the job, because (*Fortune*, January 10, 2000) the Board had lost confidence in his leadership.

As *Fortune* put it, "But for all his brilliance he somehow failed to grasp the vital quality that Goizueta had in abundance; that ethereal thing called lead-ership… Anyone can get to a certain level. But very few can function well in the really rare air. Doug was simply unable to give people a sense of pur-pose or direction."

Leaders appear in all walks of life. "It was my first encounter with a charis-matic leader. Crichton-Miller was treated by his staff and by his pupils as though he possessed superhuman powers. How far this charisma reflected the needs of his followers rather than any special quality of his own, I am not sure. The public school community of adolescents and those who choose to spend their lives educating them seems to generate a desire for inspirational leadership which is distinct from managerial competence. Per-haps this is why the idea of training headmasters has never been taken seri-ously and why selection committees rely so much on intuition." (Rae, 1993, p.33)

Rae is describing one of the headmasters he had served under (his words) as a young teacher. His comment is perceptive in that it recognises the role that followers play in determining whether a leader has "charisma" or not. Conger and Kanungo (Conger, 1988) developed a theory of charismatic leadership based on the assumption that charisma is an attributional phe-nomenon, i.e. a leader only has charisma if his followers think he has.

## Leadership is Neutral

This raises an important issue in relation to leadership, which is that it is a neutral process. Neutral in respect to morality.

No matter how we look at it, Hitler was a very effective leader. He was an abomination as a human being who was responsible for the most vile and heinous crimes against humanity. How then can we label such a person a great leader? Put yourself in a room, turn off the light, and listen to some of Hitler's speeches. Even if you do not speak German, there is a mesmerising quality about his harangues. Even if many of them were diatribes, he nevertheless aroused a whole nation to his cause. How many other men or women could have done what he did in taking a nation along with him down a path of destruction?

So when we judge leadership, we judge how effectively and efficiently the desired outcomes have been achieved. We do not judge as part of that process whether the outcome was right or wrong, good or bad. That is a matter for another debate.

Whilst leadership is a process, nevertheless leaders are people. They are individuals. It is a person who is either a great leader or a failure, not a process. So whilst we may argue and accept the proposition that leadership is a process, we cannot avoid examining the people involved in that process. In later chapters we examine the characteristics of leaders and followers as they impact leadership, but it is also necessary to understand more about leadership as it impacts the individual.

Talleyrand, that great political survivor of the 18 and 19th centuries, very neatly encapsulated the importance of the leader, " I am more afraid of an army of 100 sheep led by a lion than an army of 100 lions led by a sheep".

## Both a Science and an Art

Leadership is both a science and an art. Recognising this enables leaders to better appreciate the situation facing them. There are many decisions that a leader takes that have to be sound, rational, and logically based. There are many other decisions that will be emotionally based and may even be illogical.

It has to be recognised that whilst leadership is partly a science, albeit an immature one, the knowledge has been gained through a series of fits and starts. Moreover, understanding the rational aspects of leadership does not necessarily make a better leader. No matter how extensive the scholarship an individual may possess, this will not guarantee leadership success.

On the other hand, there are any number of people who have never opened a book who are great leaders. Theory can help, but it may not. Understanding the mechanics of a piston engine may make you a better driver. Knowing how to apply paint will certainly not make you a great painter.

Nevertheless, knowledge is never a burden and learning as much as one can about leadership can only have an upside with very little downside. It should be obvious that the more you understand of human nature, the more you understand about effective communication, the more you understand how people work as teams, the more you understand motivation, and so, on the better leader you will be.

Whilst it is an immature science and there is still much we do not understand, we have learned an awful lot in the past 40 years, and we know quite a bit about traits, abilities and behaviour related to leadership effectiveness. We have learned more about the situational and follower characteristics that affect the leader's behaviour. We know more about charisma and charismatic leaders. Despite this, there is far more unknown and hence the art becomes very important.

Leaders often draw heavily on emotion to achieve their goals. They use inspiration and passion as everyday tools of trade. Emotions are a very powerful force in getting people to do what you want them to do. Emotions can be a very effective way of lifting people's performance. Take for example the "pep talks" given by sporting coaches. These have one purpose and one purpose only: to enhance the chance of winning.

As we will see later, one of the roles of the leader is to "coach". Whereas on the football field the need to get the players "psyched up" may be obvious, it is just as necessary to get the employees of a company "psyched up", if the goal is to achieve extraordinary results.

It is fairly certain Jim Jones, on 18 November 1978, did not use reason and logic to convince 900 of his followers to commit suicide, to either drink poison or be shot, in Guyana (if in fact they did commit suicide). He is much more likely to have preyed on their emotions—their fears, their beliefs, their yearnings, their sorrows and disappointments. Hitler very much preyed on the emotions of the German people.

David Koresh, on 19 April 1993, undoubtedly convinced his Branch Davidians at Waco, Texas during the 51 day siege, not to go out to the waiting FBI, not on the basis of logical reasoning, but on emotional appeals, and 96 people died.

Emotions can have a pronounced effect on attitudes, on perceptions, and on bias. As leadership is all about taking risks, creating change, being dynamic, being creative, and getting commitment to a vision, the mental set of the followers is very relevant. Effective leaders are very sensitive to the power of appealing to the emotions—for King, God, and Country can be a rousing clarion call as the ramparts are stormed.

## Generalist or Specialist

In business in Australia there has been a long-standing myth that the CEO must be steeped in the industry. You cannot possibly run a mining company unless you have been a miner. You cannot run a bank unless you have served your apprenticeship in a branch in Cunnamulla. Look at the criticism of John Fletcher when he became CEO of Coles Myer—no retailing experience (perhaps the subsequent performance of the company justified the criticism).

I struck this when I joined a large insurance company in the early 70's as a senior executive, a deputy to the CEO. When it became clear that I was going to be a contender for the top job, the argument quickly surfaced that my lack of experience in the insurance industry was an insurmountable obstacle, or at the least a major deficiency. I argued strongly against what I considered a nonsense point of view, with little effect. I left to start a retail bank—and I knew nothing about banking, but it turned out to be a great success.

I have always believed that the CEO role has some very clear responsibilities that have nothing specifically to do with the industry in which the company operates or with the company itself. I argue, and have always argued, that a good CEO will run an airline, a bank, a mining company, or whatever, equally effectively. There are plenty of examples to support this view.

The CEO's role is to –
1.     Create and communicate the vision for the organisation.
2.     Put the right management team in place, and this includes rewarding the effective and replacing the ineffective.
3.     Establish the culture.
4.     Develop the strategy.
5.     Set big hairy audacious goals (BHAGS)
6.     Allocate resources.
7.     Monitor performance.

None of these require a lifetime spent in the industry or the company.

The role is, in my opinion, a generalist one in that sense. It is a specialist one in that being a CEO is itself a specialist role. In fact, rather than not being a disadvantage, I am firmly of the view that OTCOTI (outside the company outside the industry) is a positive advantage.

I have always been surprised at the narrow and blinkered view of many people who have spent their working life in one company or in a specific industry. They often find it difficult to think outside the square. Coming in from the outside brings a whole new perspective to bear. I have always found it exciting to explore a new company or industry, and question all those things that are accepted as being the things to do and the way to do them.

For example, when I became CEO of what was then Australia's largest home-building company, I asked why we sold our houses uninsured. The immediate response was that insurance was not our business. Our business was building houses. Yet, we all knew the first thing any homebuyer did was insure the house. I also knew (from my insurance background) that the lapse rate on house insurance policies was very low, i.e., most people automatically renewed with their existing insurer. The original writer of the policy gets a commission every time the policy is renewed—for doing absolutely nothing. The money just turns up in the bank.

At that stage we were building 5,000 houses a year in Australia, so we are talking millions of dollars in commissions compounding over the years. We would include the cover in the price, sign agency agreements with major insurers, and create a whole, new, very profitable income stream. Money for jam, but in the 60-year history of the company no one had ever thought of it, because they saw their business as building houses. In the same vein, I also stated a finance subsidiary so we could provide mortgage finance to the buyers.

Another example with the same company was what I saw as a potential acquisition opportunity. A large national company that provided security and fire protection services was the target. After doing the relevant analyses and investigations, it stacked up well as an acquisition. When I put it to the board, the first reaction was why would a construction company want to take over a security and fire protection company.

To a man (and they were all men), the very experienced and eminent directors saw this as a conflict without any synergies at all. I put it to them that there was another way of looking at the businesses. The target company outsourced all their services to sub-contractors. We, as Australia's largest homebuilder, built our houses using sub-contractors. We had been building houses for over 60 years using subcontractors and were very experienced in managing them. I put it to the board that in fact both companies were in the very same business: managing subcontractors. It was a completely different way of looking at the vital question: What business are we in? But it was too radical for the board and we did not proceed.

I believe very strongly in the generalist philosophy. In recent times in Australia, in large companies, it has become the practice, but the narrower specialist view still prevails very much in most companies. It is a view that is not prevalent in the United States.

It is interesting to note that with the merger of BHP and Billiton, much was made of the fact that the Executive Chairman of Billiton, Brian Gilbertson, who became (for a short time) CEO when Paul Anderson, the current CEO departed at the end of 2002, was "a BHP outsider". (*The Australian Financial Review*, 24 March 2001). The article goes on to comment "the explosion of the… cross-industry CEO hiring reflects a massive change in the way that big companies are choosing executive talent. Once the tried and true formula for climbing to the top of the corporate heap was to accept all challenges, work long hours and display unwavering loyalty to the company… But the old formula has been scrapped. Corporate loyalty and detailed inside industry knowledge are now merely peripheral criteria for selecting the CEO."

"The country's leading CEO headhunters say the shift in board preferences from company specific or industry specialists to one-size-fits-all CEOs with a generic set of skills began in earnest in about 1995 and has been accelerating ever since." This shift in board preference is supposedly being driven by a desire for better return on shareholders' equity. Whilst this pressure has been most noticeable on the bigger public companies, it is still not the norm for the rest.

There have been several appointments in recent years in major companies which reflect the generalist approach. As CEO of health care and logistics group Mayne Nickless, having worked in Shell (petroleum) and being CEO of Colonial (life assurance and funds management) at the time he was hired, Peter Smedley subsequently failed and left.

Telstra, until mid 2005, was headed by a former nuclear physicist and photographic film specialist (Dr. Ziggy Switowski). It is interesting that his replacement (Sol Trujillo) is an American with considerable experience in telecommunications. Westpac, until recently (2008), was headed by a former Treasury mandarin (Dr. David Morgan) who never approved a loan or filled in a passbook, and has proved to be a success.

Cable & Wireless Optus was headed by a former journalist and newspaper editor (Chris Anderson). Australia's biggest life company, AMP, was headed by a former chartered accountant (Paul Batchelor) who later worked for a bank and ran a stationery business.

CSR, the sugar milling and building materials group, was headed by a former paint industry specialist (Richard Kirby). Tabcorp was headed by a former beer baron (Ross Wilson). John Fairfax, newspaper publishing group, was headed by a former management school academic (Fred Hilmer).

The issue raised its head in relation to the higher education sector with a comment in *The Australian* of 15 March 2006, where it was remarked that universities were increasingly recruiting leaders from business, government and even lower university ranks, rather than Deputy Vice-Chancellors, because the latter had become "too specialised". A leading recruitment specialist said, "I think some of the DVC jobs are narrow so I think we might increasingly find people planning their careers…to broaden their credentials."

James Strong, Chairman of Woolworths and IAG, and former CEO of QANTAS, has been a catalyst for change in a business career that has spanned aviation, insurance and retail, as well as the arts and motor sport. Strong has said (*The Australian,* 26 January 2006) he has charted a course of moving from one industry to another to find new challenges. "I have always been attracted to situations where the organisation or the board is looking for significant change. I love the concept of trying to be part of convincing people to move in different directions and then trying to get momentum and an acceptance of responsibility instead of opposition." This is what leaders like to do. In mid-2005, out of the top 20 companies in Australia, the CEO of eight came from outside the company. Macquarie Bank, Australia's most successful bank and dubbed the "Millionaires' Factory", clearly supports the generalist approach. In January 2006, it appointed Russell Balding, then CEO of the Australian Broadcasting Corporation (ABC), as CEO of Sydney Airport. He replaced Max Moore-Wilton who had himself been appointed some three years earlier from his post as Secretary of the Department of Prime Minister and Cabinet.

As to be expected, the Board of the Airline Representatives of Australia, the umbrella group representing Australian Airlines, said it would have preferred to have an experienced airport executive appointed. "It's just an understanding about airlines and what airports are all about that we like to see in our airport CEOs." (*The Australian*, 21 January 2006). No mention was made of the fact that, based on bottom-line results, Moore-Wilton had been a very successful CEO.

Macquarie Bank's view on the other hand, which accords with mine, extolled the virtue of Balding's financial and managerial track record.

Tabcorp, the billion dollar casino and wagering business, also apparently supports the generalist approach. Its CEO, Matthew Slatter, before going to Tabcorp was chief financial officer and director of a financial services group Axa Asia Pacific. In January 2006, he appointed a senior executive from the ANZ bank only weeks after hiring the former CEO of Arnotts Biscuits to run the casino division. It is worthwhile noting that Switkowski (mentioned above) also joined the board of Tabcorp in late 2005.

In 1999, Jacques Nasser became CEO of the Ford Motor Company. At the same time William Clay (Bill) Ford, the great-grandson of the founder, was named chairman. Two years later, Ford took over as CEO after firing Nasser, and became the first family member to run the company in 19 years.

There were a lot of critics that said an insider was a bad choice. "Any insider is the wrong person to fix a Ford or a GM. Insiders have too much of a connection to the status quo and the legacy of the company to make the tough decisions that are needed." (*Time Magazine*, 30 January, 2006, p.43)

A survey by Booz Allen Hamilton reported in *The Australian* (18 June 2005, p.34) showed that in 2004 57% of new CEOs appointed in Australia came from outside the company, compared with 40% in 2003. and only 33% in 2000.

One of the forces driving OTCOTI is globalisation. This is why it is impacting the big companies. Globalisation means that the ground rules tomorrow will be very different from yesterday. Globalisation means that tomorrow's competitors will be different from yesterday's. Globalisation means that all the experience and knowledge gained in Australia is suddenly devalued. International experience becomes the *sine qua non* of a successful CEO of a major corporation.

It really is no surprise that we are seeing a move in this direction. Success is all about giving shareholders maximum returns and the CEO's primary task is to allocate investment to the highest rate of return. That was always the CEO's role and so many Australian companies performed so badly because it was ignored. Other goals, such as size or market share, were given priority, often at the expense of profit.

I recall when I took over as CEO of one large company, I commented on the lack of percentage signs in their monthly financial reports. The point I was trying to make was that returns were fundamental. I then said that the two most important people in the company were ROSE and PAT—Return on Shareholders' Equity and Profit After Tax.

Institutional investors now take a much more active interest in company performance and are insisting on better returns. therefore, CEOs must keep their eyes focused clearly on the bottom line.

## A Journey

Most of those who attain a leadership role do so as the result of a journey. That journey may be easy or it may be difficult. It may be long, it may be short. It may be enjoyable, it may be painful. Ultimately it may be worth it, or it may not.

This journey in business often parallels the life cycle of a business. The entrepreneur conceives of the bright idea, sees an opportunity where others have not, mortgages their house and puts all at risk, because they believe passionately in their ideas. They go down the early commercialisation path, scratching for capital, selling off as little equity as possible, and slowly build a business.

The journey then enters the phase of needing to establish procedures, to introduce some order into the growing number of people involved in the business, to enter new markets, to tap new sources of capital. The business now needs a competent and experienced manager. Someone who can bring order into chaos, who will focus on introducing systems, will keep a sharp eye on the bottom line, will try to minimise risk, and generally put the business on a sound footing.

The business then reaches a plateau. It is in a mature market, it needs new products and processes, and it is stagnating. Then is the moment for a leader. Someone who will come in to the organisation with a new vision, who will energise the tired workforce, who will set new goals and new strategies, who will (if necessary) turn the organisation upside down to achieve the goals he sets.

After some time, the business might settle into a successful and growing mode which no longer requires the level of change that needs strong leadership. At this point in time many leaders seek new and more challenging pastures, and are replaced by a shepherd who will sustain and maintain the success he (the leader) created. They will do this by encouraging the staff rather than by inspiring them, by accepting the status quo and avoiding risk, by focusing on care of the people and keeping their eye on the surroundings rather than on the horizon.

Perpetual change can be as damaging to an organisation as no change at all. Judicious cycling of leaders, shepherds and managers may be the most appropriate formula for many companies, but may be anathema to others. This sort of lifecycle is perhaps best seen in some of the oldest and biggest companies, for example in the automotive industry. William Durant, the man who started General Motors (GM), was an outstanding entrepreneur who brought together a number of companies to form a conglomerate that was to become one of the world's largest companies. But he was not a manager. The man who succeeded him was a manager par excellence: Alfred P Sloan. Sloan became a byword in management literature, and the management structure and philosophy of GM became the bible for U.S. business. Sloan became a corporate legend.

Sloan introduced organisational structure, systems, procedures, and deci-sion-making mechanisms that became the bywords of many corporations until this day. But he also introduced strategy, delegation and a clear under-standing of the respective roles of boards and management. The three S's of strategy, structure and systems were Sloan's mantra.

## The View From the Grandstand

Leaders need to be able to take what is sometimes called a "helicopter" view of the situation. Leaders have to be able to see the whole tapestry as well as how the parts fit together. Without this more encompassing view, it is difficult to see where change has to be instituted.

What distinguishes the very best players on a football field from the rest is this ability to "read the game". They have the rare ability, whilst embroiled in the fury of the game on the field, at the same time to be aware of the broader movement of the game, the tactics that their opponents are using, and are able to anticipate future moves. Players with this gift almost invari-ably become captain so that they can exercise leadership on the field.

In business it is much the same. Leaders have to be able to "read" the situ-ation, identify the key issues, anticipate the likely strategies of their com-petitors, and plan their own strategy accordingly.

## Why Leaders Fail

Leaders also fail. Leaders do one of two things. They either lead or they mislead. We have seen many examples in Australia in recent years of lead-ers who have failed. It is seen quite frequently in the political field where leaders, such as Paul Keating and John Howard, stay beyond their use-by date. It is also seen in business where a leader who has been quite success-ful suddenly strikes a series of reversals and he is just as suddenly no longer a leader. Witness John Prescott of BHP, Philip Brass of Pacific Dunlop, John Spalvins of Adsteam, Bob Dalziel of Mayne Nickless, Brian Quinn and John Fletcher of Coles Myer, and many others.

In early 2001, there was speculation that Nick Falloon of PBL, Rod Chad-wick of Pacific Dunlop, Dennis Eck of Coles Myer, Eric Dodd of NRMA, Chris Anderson of CW Optus, Andrew Forrest of Anaconda Nickel, David Hearn of Goodman Fielder, Randolph Wein of HIH, Terry McCartney of Myer Grace Bros., were all on a short string. By mid-April that year Fal-loon, Chadwick, Wein, Dodd and McCartney had all gone.

When Chadwick departed Pacific Dunlop one report (*The Australian*, 1 April 2001, p.32) said, "…Chadwick is seen as a gifted manufacturer who is good at the nuts and bolts side of the business. However, many believe he lacked the leadership, charisma, and the people skills to inspire people." There is increasing recognition of the importance of leadership and what this actually means. This comment on Chadwick is an example of this.

It has to be appreciated that many people in potential leadership positions, such as a CEO, often fail because they never become leaders. This is a different kind of failure from one who has been a leader and fallen from the perch. However, oftentimes they fail for the same reasons.

Why do leaders fail? Generally, because they do not respond appropriately to a change in the situation. They do not recognise the change or else they do not know how to respond to the change.

One aspect which oftentimes trips them up is timing. Timing is critical to a leader's success and to their failure. Many would-be leaders never realise their potential, because their particular skills were not the ones required when the opportunity arose. Winston Churchill is a supreme example of this. Had he died in 1939 at the age of sixty-five, he would have had a far different obituary than when he died in 1965 at the age of 92, revered as the greatest Englishman of the 20th Century. It is worthwhile remembering that Winston's father, Lord Randolph Churchill, was a brilliant political failure who died at the early age of 46, after ruining his own political career.

Failure does not necessarily mean incompetence or lack of ability. It may be nothing more than lack of opportunity. Failure to become prime minister for many is just that. Who would have predicted that William Hague or Tony Blair would have become leaders of their respective political parties in the United Kingdom?

Oftentimes it is not so much failure as disappointment. Coming second in the race for the top job in an organisation is not a failure. Sure it is a disappointment (remember the aphorism at the beginning of the chapter), but it is not a failure. Both disappointment and failure should be seen as an opportunity. For many it has been the defining moment in a career. It may result in moving on to something new. It may result in a reassessment of goals and objectives. It may strengthen resolve and determination to succeed.

Failure is not always the end of the line. It is often the motivation for subsequent success. Churchill is such an example. In 80 test innings Don Bradman scored seven ducks (0 runs), including his last test innings, but also achieved an average of 99.94, the next best player average being 60.97 (but over 41 innings).

Kouzes and Posner (1995, p.69) give some interesting examples of where failure was a precursor to success. Babe Ruth struck out 1,330 times. In between he hit 714 home runs. Martina Navratilova lost 21 of her first 24 matches against Chris Evert, then won 39 out of the next 57 matches. R H Macy failed in retailing seven times before his store in New York became a success. Abraham Lincoln failed twice as a businessman and was defeated in six state and national elections before being elected President of the United States. Theodor S (Dr. Seuss) Geisel's first children's book was rejected by 23 publishers. The 24th publisher sold six million copies.

Coming to grips with disappointment or failure and using it as a learning experience is usually beneficial to the person concerned. Leaders in business sometimes find this quite difficult. Business encourages a logical analytical approach to problem solving and decision-making. CEOs and senior executives do have egos and are generally not disposed to a lot of self-doubt and self-analysis. It is important in their role that they are in fact confident and self-assured. Consequently, the emotional domain of their personality is often subordinated to the analytical, to the detriment of the former.

Intuition and empathy are valuable assets for a leader. Understanding how others feel, to know what they value, to instinctively be able to appeal to them, are what makes leaders successful. In the Western macho male leadership arena this is not a widespread skill in men. It exists much more in women, who are far more ready to explore and respond to feelings. Men are supposed to take action rather than engage with their feelings. Even today, when men see no issue with crying in public, many men would regard being "shell-shocked" as a feeble excuse for avoiding action rather than a condition to be treated. It would rank just behind desertion as something to be punished.

As a consequence, many men in business have poorly adjusted emotional lives. The office becomes their refuge as well as the focus of their energies. We read from time to time leading businessmen such as Peter Ritchie, Chairman of McDonald's, baring their soul and talking of the price they have paid in their personal lives for this all-devouring attention to business.

We see this emotional conflict exhibited in any number of ways. Rare is the middle-aged businessman whose second wife is not younger or more glamorous than his first. Frequent is the arrogance of the political or business leader who refuses to listen to advice, or fails to admit to mistakes, or fails to see that his time has come.

Suppressing emotions may well be a requirement during the single-mindedness of the managerial phase, but it is a severe disadvantage as a leader. Suppressing emotions as a leader can lead to dangerous situations. Leaders in such situations can start believing their own myths, can regard themselves as invincible, and even worse indispensable, and can take decisions which reflect their own infallibility.

Leaders are not always moderate, balanced, thoughtful, or careful articulators of policy. Some are in many respects part of the lunatic fringe, in their passionate belief in their own very good idea. Leaders tend to fail in stages. The first tends to follow success, particularly a period of sustained success. The leader suddenly finds that he is being feted. He reads of his success in the media. He is interviewed and asked for the reasons for his genius. He is in demand as a speaker. He starts to lose his grip on reality and oftentimes starts to focus on new interests which hitherto had been out of his ken. Frequently, this is sexual. Power, status and money are strong aphrodisiacs.

He now enters the second phase. He stops listening to his advisers. His inflated ego prevents him from seeing the reality of the situation. Worse still, he begins to listen to those in his new circle who do not know anything about the business. At the same time, he sees the advice from his original advisers as trying to undermine him. He becomes isolated and remote. He becomes more and more difficult to communicate with.

The third and terminal phase is when his board loses confidence in him. He is unable to convince the board that he has a strategy for recovery. He is opposing the recommendations from his own management team. It is clear to the board, but not to him, that he is no longer in control. He decides to "pursue other interests". Exit stage left.

# CHAPTER 8 -

# Those Behind

*If you're not prepared to trust others, why trust yourself?*

## An Essential Part of the Equation

Followers are an essential part of the leadership equation. I mentioned at the beginning that I am often struck by the fact that many people think that by looking in the mirror they see a leader. What they need to realise is that if there is no one else in the mirror, they are not leading.

One cannot be a leader without followers. It is not a solo role. It may be solitary, lonely, friendless, isolated or whatever, but it is not solo. Without his armies, Napoleon was just a little Frenchman with grandiose ambitions.

One of my central theses is that leadership is a process and not a position or a role. Being the CEO, a 4-star general, the pope, or the prime minister does not make you a leader. Most of us have seen many examples of just the opposite. A common complaint about people in such positions is that they "lack leadership".

Leadership is a complex series of interactions between the leader, the followers and the situation. It is the interplay of all of these factors that give leadership the infinite variations that make it impossible to predict the outcome. Similarly, followership is not a person but a role, and what distinguishes followers from leaders is not the individual, but the role they play. One moment one may be an effective leader, the next an effective follower.

Followers, therefore, are just as important in leadership as the leader. And yet many texts on leadership barely mention followers. It seems that leadership is merely about the leader. The discussion dwells on leaders' characteristics, their attributes, their personal qualities, their charisma or lack of it, the quality of their decisions, their leadership styles and so on.

These are certainly important in understanding leadership , but one cannot overlook that all of these things are affected by and influenced by the followers. Different followers will create different situations. What may well be the right decision with one group of followers may well be disaster with a different set of followers.

## The Importance of Understanding

One of the skills necessary in leadership is the ability to understand the followers—their attitudes, their skill sets, their values, their preferences, their needs, their desires, and their willingness to do what is required.

Effective leaders will be sensitive to all these issues and more, and the depth of their understanding and empathy will play a large part in their success or otherwise as a leader. Some leaders have given followers a bad name. The Pied Piper and Hitler, for example, depict followers as simpleminded automatons who will blindly follow. Certainly at times the result can be disaster—take lemmings as an example.

Most of us spend the greater part of our lives as followers, but we concentrate on that small part during which we might lead, or shepherd, or manage. From our early childhood, through school, in sport, at work, we are generally in the situation of being followers. So followership dominates our lives. Just as many people are not good leaders, so many followers are not good followers.

There are many examples which demonstrate the importance of followers and the critical role they can play in an organisation or even in a nation. Therefore, it not only behooves leaders to pay close attention to their followers, but their leadership is also likely to improve the more they understand about followers and their importance in the leadership equation.

When we accept the inescapable conclusion that leadership is about people, we recognise that those people are followers. Leaders need to continually upgrade their team. I will talk about teams later.

Leaders need to be constantly coaching, evaluating and building self-confidence in their followers. There is little doubt that the team with the best players usually does win, so a large proportion of the leader's time and effort has to be put into building the competence of the team. Self-confidence energises. Good leaders establish confidence in themselves amongst their followers. Great leaders establish self-confidence in their followers.

Constant encouragement, care and recognition are an essential part of leadership. Jack Welch had a neat way of putting it. "Think of yourself as a gardener, a watering can in one hand and fertiliser in the other." He says that now and again you have to pull some weeds, but most of the time, you just nurture and tend. Then everything blooms. When we see leadership in these terms, we then recognise the nonsense of yearly performance reviews. Performance review and evaluation is a constant daily activity, and feedback should be just as frequent. Good leaders let their followers know how they are performing on a continuing basis.

I always told my staff they should never go to bed wondering whether they were doing a good job or not. They would know, because that was the culture of the organisation. Periodic formal reviews can and do serve other purposes, but as far as performance is concerned no one should have to wait until some sort of formal review to know whether their performance was satisfactory or not.

Hand in hand with this must be total trust and confidence in the leader. People should always know where they stand. And if they do not trust leadership, it is not possible to achieve this level of confidence. This means that the bad news has to come with the good. Trying to gild the lily is not only foolish and deceitful; it will destroy trust. Tell it how it is.

There is a phrase used in American business (I have not heard it used in Australia) that you don't kiss up and kick down, because people should be self-confident enough to know that their performance or the performance of their team will get them recognition. In bad times, like the Charge of the Light Brigade, leaders take responsibility for failure. In good times, like the Battle of Britain, they praise the troops.

Tough calls are tough because they affect people. I always said that it was much easier to start a new business or division than to close one down. That might seem obvious, but it is amazing just how long some executives will keep a business going, long after it should have been axed.

The leaders' job is to explain the reasons behind the tough decisions so that people can see the logic and reasons for them. Transparency is a very valuable tool in getting tough decisions accepted. Leaders are there to lead. They are not there to win a popularity contest (even in politics). In business, a leader does not have to run for office. They are already elected, so honesty is paramount.

There are good followers and there are bad followers. And it is interesting to note that many of the characteristics and the skill set that go to make effective leaders are also necessary for good followers. Many make the quite deliberate decision to be followers rather than leaders, for a whole variety of reasons , but one of the most common reasons is a different tolerance to risk.

Just as risk and a person's attitude to risk is one of the main differentiating factors between leaders, shepherds, managers and entrepreneurs, so too does it often determine whether a person wants to be a follower or a leader. Being a follower usually requires taking less risk than a leader. It requires less exposure to the vicissitudes of life.

One of the main differences between man and animal is the willingness of the former to take risks. Animals generally do not knowingly and willingly risk their lives. Man is prepared to do so if the potential reward is considered to be worth it.

Leaders inspire risk-taking by setting the example. Leaders urge their people to try new things and do not whack them in the head when they fail. Leaders have to get rid of the NIH (not invented here) syndrome, which stifles experimentation.

Risk-taking is also about learning. If you do not try, you may never know. Followers are people and people enjoy celebrating. Celebrating success helps create an atmosphere of recognition and positive energy. Leaders need to make a big deal out of successes. If they do not, no one will.

In the same category is how leaders expect staff to manage work and family, and I emphasise that it is an issue that has to be managed by the individual. Leaders set the culture, but people have to manage within that culture. It is therefore important that leaders establish a culture that is supportive of a rewarding work-life balance.

Early in 2005, Allens Arthur Robinson won an award conducted by the *Business Review Weekly* as the best large law firm and large professional services firm of the year, based on the views of clients. The firm is a full-service commercial law firm with offices in Sydney, Melbourne, Brisbane, Perth, Beijing, Shanghai, Hong Kong, Bangkok, Singapore, Jakarta, Phnom Penh, Port Moresby. It had 190 partners and a staff of 1,500.

Tom Poulton, the Managing Partner, is the first to admit that working for Allens Arthur Robinson is no picnic and had this to say, "We don't run this place as a holiday camp ... We expect our people to treat the client as if they were God and to put themselves out for clients. You don't say 'Sorry I can't do it, I'm playing cricket on the weekend'... **You don't have a right to any free time.**" (my emphasis) As to be expected, this drew some very critical comments. This is not the work-life balance I would support, and in fact I think it is a very silly statement. Recent (2008) comment in the press would indicate that the large legal firms are finding it increasingly difficult to convince staff to accept partnerships because of the level of commitment (time) required.

### What Makes a Good Follower?

As with leaders, one of the essential characteristics of a good follower is integrity. Integrity is non-negotiable. People with integrity tell the truth. They keep their word and they can be trusted. People with integrity are courageous, honest and credible. Secondly, they need to be intelligent. One of my first bosses in the Postmaster General's Department gave me invaluable advice when he said, "Always make sure you recruit people smarter than yourself." He had just recruited me, so he made me feel good.

Intelligence is not just mental prowess. They need to have insatiable curiosity. A willingness, nay a burning need, to ask questions. They need to be able to work with or lead other just as intelligent people. They need to be independent, critical thinkers.

Thirdly, they must have broad shoulders, an ability to handle stress and setbacks; and to handle them with grace and dignity, and in the same way to handle success with joy and humility.

Jack Welch used to use what he called the "4-E and 1-P Framework". The first E is positive energy. To thrive on action and relish change. The second

E is the ability to energise others, and inspire them to take on the impossible. The third E is edge. The courage to make tough yes or no decisions. The fourth E is execute. The ability to get jobs done. The final P is passion. What he calls a heartfelt, deep and authentic excitement about work.

Good followers can succeed without strong leadership. Leaders can safely delegate to good followers. Good followers often become more like business partners. Treat them as equals. One of my best senior executives followed me from the first company I hired him in, through two of my subsequent moves, each in very different industries, and very different executive roles. And he succeeded in all of them. He eventually became a very successful entrepreneur. He remains a good friend to this day.

Good followers do not have to be driven. Sometimes they have to be reined in, but leaders should have no problem with that. They will take on extra work gladly, they will upgrade their skills, and they will solve problems unasked. I always found it better to have to rein enthusiastic people in, rather than having to apply a hot poker to liven them up.

Most organisations assume that leadership has to be taught, but that everyone knows how to follow. Educating followers can be just as important.

## Teams

Just a word on teams. One of the features of recent management literature has been a focus on "teams" versus "groups". Teams and teamwork were the buzz words of the 1990s.

A group is defined as two or more individuals who interact with each other and are interdependent in some way. Time might be added in that groups have a past, a present and a future. We might say that it is a collection of people who perceive themselves to be one.

Teams share the same characteristics, plus they have one additional critical component. Teams exist for some task-oriented purpose. Teams have explicit goals and team members are aware of these goals. The difference between groups and teams is that teams have shared goals. We might say, therefore, that a team is a group of people who share common objectives and need to work together to achieve them.

We know the old adage of a champion team will always beat a team of champions. All this might seem obvious, but leaders have to be sensitive to whether they have a group or a team of followers. It will make all the difference between success and failure. It also helps if leaders understand a little of the psychology of groups so that they are aware of and understand concepts such as social loafing, social facilitation, group think, intra-group conflict, group roles, group norms, communication networks, group cohesion, and so on.

A little anecdote on group norms. One of the norms for many groups, e.g. the military, bike gangs, police services, etc., is the style and manner of dress. It is interesting to note that the successful law firm mentioned above had, in the previous year (2004), abolished its casual-Friday policy, which allowed staff to dress down at the end of each week.

Poulton said: "It occurred to us that the casual-Friday phenomenon might in fact be giving rise to a general laxness of standards on Fridays - near enough is good enough - and a feeling that we just didn't need to care as much with the weekend looming. Our staff were initially unhappy about this, but the simple fact is that it worked. Our partners and staff know that it is never acceptable to slacken off in their client service ethic."

The bottom line is that leaders should strive to not only develop teams, but successful teams. Research has identified some characteristics identified with successful teams. Leaders would do well to understand these.

1. Effective teams have a clear mission.
2. Effective teams have high performance standards.
3. Leaders of successful teams take constant stock of resources available.
4. Good leaders work to secure the resources necessary for team effectiveness.
5. Good leaders spend considerable time assessing the competence of team members.
6. Leaders of effective teams spend considerable time planning and organising.
7. High levels of communication are associated with effective teams.
8. Minimum levels of interpersonal conflict.

As I said above, the importance of followers seems to have been undervalued. They play a key role in success and leaders need to realise this. They are an essential part of the equation.

# CHAPTER 9 -

# The Situation

*The real test of honesty is lying to yourself.*

## The Relevance of the Organisation

In the process that we describe as leadership, the situation is probably the most complex of the three components. As it is a process, another way of looking at leadership is as an outcome ; the outcome of the interaction between the leader, the followers, and the situation. Whilst the situation includes all the external factors that impinge upon the process in train, the organisation is often the central feature in the situation, especially in the business context.

A leader can be successful in one organisation, but fail in another. It is too simplistic to attribute the failure to the organisation, because there are numerous other aspects that would have changed as well. But because the organisation is so central in the process, it can have a significant impact on the outcome. The organisation, and the very nature of the organisation, can have a determining influence on the outcome, that is on the leadership.

The question has to be asked: Can an organisation develop a leadership culture? The answer is yes, insofar as the culture of the organisation can positively enhance the emergence of leadership rather than constrain it. Or to put it another way, it can reinforce the emergence of leaders rather than managers, shepherds or entre(intra)preneurs.

Whilst we know that a leader may be successful in one organisation and fail in another, we also know that many organisations succeed under different leaders. Why is this so? An organisation is a combination of people, systems and processes. This mix can help to create a favourable culture for leaders and leadership to emerge.

It is quite obvious that in a large organisation such as GE, Jack Welch cannot be personally responsible for its every decision and every success. He would certainly not claim to be. What is it in the organisation that delivers success after success? Perhaps a more relevant question in this context is: How does the organisation deliver success after success?

In Chapter 10, I refer to the organisational culture needed to build on a central idea at every opportunity. This is what I call "Strategic IQ". Clearly an organisation that has developed Strategic IQ has positioned itself to effectively meet competitive challenges. This is all about behaviour and performance. When we link this to the argument that leadership is something that exists or can exist at all levels in an organisation, we begin to see how successful leaders can build an organisation that has the capacity to generate outcomes that buttress leadership.

## The Importance of Culture

Every leadership act takes place somewhere, sometime, and the act is affected by, and influenced by, those factors. This is the "situation". In battle, generals try to choose the time, place and conditions that will best suit their strategy. In business, the time, place and conditions for a new product launch, or the announcement of a take-over bid for a company, are carefully selected to optimise the outcome.

Some uncaring leaders give little thought to these aspects when they are dealing with people issues. Giving an employee a pink slip (dismissal) on Christmas Eve is not only soul destroying for the affected employee, but it also sends a clear message to the organisation as to the sort of culture that exists in that organisation. The attitude will be, "If they can do it to Fred, they can do it to me." And culture is a defining characteristic of every organisation. Culture is not something that just happens in an organisation. It does not emerge from a darkened room. It does not grow from the bottom up. It is imposed from the top down. And I use the word "imposed" quite deliberately.

One of the most important tasks of a CEO is to create, instill and sustain the culture of the organisation. And this has to be done by establishing from the outset the sorts of behaviour that are acceptable, the sorts of outcomes that are desired, the values that are applicable and those that are not, the attitudes that are expected, the level of performance that is needed, the results that are demanded, and the general standard of how people, be they customers, colleagues, competitors, suppliers or whoever are treated.

The CEO of Heinz Australia, Peter Widdow, credits changes in organisational culture for making Heinz a better company. (*Manangement Today*, Nov/Dec 2008, p7) Widdow describes the culture of the company he took over as "negative", "punitive", "aggressive". He said there was not any "nurturing","positivity","engagement". He also makes the point that the changes have to occur quickly.

The literature today is very much oriented towards the teamwork, cooperative, consensus, and participative style of leadership. It tends to denigrate the autocratic, directive style of years gone by. It has, in some respects, gone too far in this criticism. It is not fashionable to admit to it, but there are many occasions when the most appropriate form of leadership is autocratic, direct, no-nonsense, unambiguous instructions as to what you want done. This clearly applies(necessarily so) in the military.

Many CEOs who profess the current mantra of participative leadership are frequent practitioners of the table thumping, loud, demanding, presumptive style they pretend not to be, and oftentimes surprisingly and disappointedly liberally peppered with profanities. All you have to do to see them in action is to get into their inner sanctum.

Is it reasonable to "demand" anything in these days of consensus and compromise? Should leaders "demand" levels of performance or should they be less forceful and aggressive? Of course there is no one answer, and the only answer can be: whatever works the best.

The point I am making, however, is that there are occasions when a very clear, unambiguous demand is the best approach, and leaders should not be frightened to use this approach—without apologies. Jack Welch said, "If you want to instill enthusiasm for an idea in 240,000 people, you can't be soft and gentle. To some extent, you have to be an extremist."(Lowe, p.184)

Culture may be explained in words, it may be expressed in memos, it may be proclaimed in speeches, but it will only be instilled by action. "Do as I do, not do as I say," has to be the guiding principle as far as the leader is concerned. In the heat of battle this may be by personal acts of bravery to give example to others to follow. It may be by bearing hardship without complaint. It may be by eating in the cafeteria and not the executive dining room. It may be by abolishing the executive dining room. It may be by giving up the reserved parking.

Whatever it is, there has to be a clear message from leaders in what they do that communicates the culture they want. Gerry Harvey, the founder of Harvey Norman and one of the most successful retailers in Australia, knows the importance of culture and he knows where it comes from. Harvey believes that customer service has to come from within: "It's about changing the culture of an organisation... You've got to have the culture there and the change has to come from the top." (*Management Today*, Jan/Feb 2005, p.121).

Leaders have to decide the culture they want in the organisation. They then have to embed it and continuously reinforce it. How do they do this?

Leaders communicate their priorities, values and concerns in a variety of ways. They do this by what they ask about, by how they measure things (especially performance), by what they comment on, by what they praise, by what they criticise. A particularly important signal of their values is whom they appoint, promote and dismiss. Another particularly effective means of communication is by emotional displays. These may be anger, joy, sorrow, regret, annoyance, or other emotional displays.

Colin Powell (U.S. Secretary of State and Chairman of the Joint Chiefs of Staff) tells a wonderful story of when he was on the staff of a general who wanted to send a birthday card to each soldier in his command on their birthday and instructed Powell to implement the system. Powell did not think much of the idea and did not follow it up. Subsequently, the general asked Powell how the system was working and Powell had to admit he had not implemented it. The general reacted by softly saying, "Shucks Colin, I wished you had."

Powell said he went out and immediately did so, and felt ashamed he had not done so earlier. That was that particular general's emotional reinforcement of the culture he wanted. It was very effective. Another general may have well shouted and thumped the table, and that may have been just as effective. There is no one best way.

The significance of culture in the leadership equation is generally recognised. In the *The Australian Financial Review* for example (on 4 March 2005), in a story on possible changes in the CEOs of the major banks in Australia it said, "...to confront the key issue of succession planning and what a change of CEOs may mean for the strategy, culture and leadership..."

One reason leaders love crises is that a crisis is a wonderful opportunity to instill and reinforce values and culture. Crises are very emotional times and the environment enhances the potential for learning about values and what is expected of people. Crises give leaders the opportunity to demonstrate to the whole organisation what they believe to be the important issues and how they expect people to behave.

In the political arena, Peter Beattie, a Premier of Queensland, is a good example of a leader who not only survives crises, but thrives on them. A series of crises over several years provided Beattie with opportunities to demonstrate strong, decisive leadership, which then allowed him to implement policies that gave him a stronger connection with the electorate. In this sense he is a "transformational" leader rather than a "transactional" leader. But without these crises, Beattie would just be another "transactional" politician.

Leaders have to realise that they are role models. People watch how they behave, what they say, what they do, how they dress, and how they talk. They take notice of their working habits, their level of commitment to their job, service beyond the call of duty, and self sacrifice. They take particular notice of whether their actions match their rhetoric. Leadership is about do what I do, not do what I say.

Leaders could learn a lot from St. Francis of Assisi who said, **"Preach the Gospel; if necessary, use words."**

Leaders could benefit from an understanding of Confucian philosophy. Confucius' political philosophy is rooted in the belief that a ruler should learn self-discipline, should govern subjects by his own example, and should treat them with love and concern. He advised: "The moral character of the ruler is the wind; the moral character of those beneath him is the grass. When the wind blows, the grass bends."

Rewards and punishments are useful techniques for reinforcing culture. Rewards can come in many forms: promotion, cash, recognition (such as employee of the month), special privileges and so on.

Organisational structures, processes, systems and procedures all help to communicate the culture of the organisation. Formal budgets, performance reviews, planning sessions, executive development programs, office layout, formal statements of values, missions, philosophies all help to reinforce the culture the leader is trying to instill and nurture.

An effective but often neglected way of communicating values is by way of "war stories". Stories about important events and people in the organisation, recounting of past incidents which illustrate the sort of organisation it is, stories of characters who have been in the organisation and typify its values. All of these are very effective ways in which to get staff to better understand just what is important in the organisation.

It is easy to dismiss the importance of culture in the success of an organisation, but good leaders know how critical it can be. In early 2006, Lakshmi Mittal, the Indian-born chairman of the world's biggest steel producer, Mittal Steel, made a hostile takeover bid of US$22.6 billion for Europe's biggest steel company, Arcelor, based in Luxembourg, whose CEO is Guy Dolle.

When Dolle was asked about a possible merger option by Mittal, he said he replied neither yes nor no. "I just said 75% to 80% of mergers fail because of cultural differences." (*TIME*, February 13, 2006, p.28) The bid caused a furore in Europe, because it was viewed as a rough attempt by "new" India to take on "old" Europe.

Dick Clark, the head of drug giant Merck, said "The fact is culture eats strategy for lunch….you can have good strategy but if you don't have the culture and enabling systems to implement that staatregy……you will fail (*The Australian Financial Review*, 31 March 2006, p.96)

## SGIO Building Society (now Suncorp)

When we established (in 1977) the SGIO (State Government Insurance Office) Building Society (a savings and loans bank), as CEO I made it clear that I wanted a particular image of customer friendliness and efficiency, with a distinct image vis-à-vis our competitors.

Staff dealing with the public were provided with uniforms, male staff had to wear ties, tellers could not have stools (as they were required to stand) whilst serving customers, and chewing gum, smoking, eating or drinking at the counter was not allowed. That might seem draconian today, but there was no doubt in everybody's mind what was required. And whilst some of this might be common today, in the late 70's it was not.

On the other hand, staff were given every assistance and training to be able to provide the best possible service to their customers, and they were encouraged to treat them as THEIR customers—get to know them, call them by name, ask about their families and so on. They were given the products, the systems, and the support to make them feel proud of what they were doing and the organisation they were working for. Our advertising campaigns, slogans such as "As Close as a Smile Away", were all designed to reinforce the culture. We had very low staff turnover, morale was high, and for the seven years I was CEO we grew the business at three times the rate of the rest of the industry every year.

We created a culture that said very clearly to the market that we were customer friendly. We saw our business as being to help them with their financial dealings. We kept our products and our systems simple to promote customer friendliness. We led the market with several innovations that have become commonplace in banking today. For seven years we met a target I set of one new product per month. I personally contributed by identifying new products and services. I wanted to demonstrate it was everybody's challenge.

Leaders have to be mindful that every act, every decision, will be measured against the culture being imposed. The sort of people appointed to particular jobs will either reinforce or weaken the culture. The reasons why people are promoted or dismissed will either strengthen the culture or weaken it. How people are treated by others will send a message.

Unless leaders reinforce the culture with every act and decision, it will not be as strong and as all pervasive as it should be. The importance of culture in an organisation cannot be overemphasized. It is one of the main drivers in the business. How often have you dealt with a business and wished the people were more friendly, more sympathetic, more efficient or just more interested in you as a customer? (Don't you just love the impersonal service of call centres?)

Leaders like chaos. They welcome ambiguity. The reason is very simple. In a situation of uncertainty there is an unequalled opportunity to effect change. Leaders are not interested in the status quo. The status quo provides no opportunity for change. If there is no sense of uncertainty, leaders will often deliberately manufacture one, for then they have the environment to effect change, and one of the prime targets of change will be the culture of the organisation.

It is much easier to create a culture than it is to change a culture. In a large organisation or an organisation in which a culture has been entrenched for a long time, it may take years for CEOs to effect the changes they want. In describing how this should be achieved there is far too much unrealistic emphasis in the theory on the consensus and handholding approach.

In business there is frequently the need to demand, direct, impose, enforce or whatever word we want to use to get the result desired. Good leadership is strong leadership, and staff react favourably to leaders who make it very clear in no uncertain terms what is expected of them. Equivocation and uncertainty are corrosive to effective leadership.

## QANTAS

Qantas CEO James Strong, regarded generally as an effective CEO, in *The Age* on 12 October 2000, while discussing turning a corporate culture upside down is reported as saying that to be successful you need a realistic view on people's receptivity and time, plenty of it. He said that it could take three to five years to get an organisation solidly on the reform path. He has a reputation for speaking bluntly and intimately to his staff.

In the early days of his being CEO at Qantas there was much blood-letting in the senior ranks as he brought in from outside Qantas his own team of senior executives. But having done that he quickly settled in to his preferred role as a transformational leader and coach.

Qantas had been government owned and until Strong arrived, and he was a board member at the time of his appointment as CEO having previously been CEO of TAA, another government-owned airline, it still had the culture of a government instrumentality. There had been previous attempts to change the culture which had failed, and there were many who predicted he would also fail and the airline itself would not survive long. He has proved them wrong. He referred to the need for compulsion. "You can change people's minds (through talk) but until you force it nothing happens."

Strong described how he had spent four years trying to bring in a restructuring of airport operations. People agreed to change methods at negotiations, but nothing ever came of it until Qantas told all staff their positions would be put to tender and they would have to compete in groups to keep their old jobs. Each group of workers won their places back against outside tenderers and the experience was transformational.

Whereas previously much energy was devoted to union and management attempts to outfox each other, the new situation saw staff focusing on key indicators and feeling they had ownership of their areas. He said the new model for the airline was built on a mixture of "concern and confidence" — confidence among the staff that their positions were secure if they performed, but concern that they had to keep performing to remain securely employed. He regularly shared his vision for the company with his employees and where possible dealt with them in small groups, enthusing and inspiring them from the front.

Dexter Dunphy, professor at the University of Technology, Sydney is very complimentary: "His time at Qantas has been marked by a remarkably successful and continuous change program incorporating significant cultural change. James Strong is one of the most flexible CEOs and agents of change in Australia—his ability to alter his style of change management from time to time is quite remarkable." (*The Australian Financial Review*, 14-15 October 2000).

## AMP

George Trumbull, the brash imported American CEO of the AMP, who was appointed by the board in 1994 and sacked by the board in 1999, almost a year before his contract was due to expire, recognised the need to change the culture of AMP when he became CEO. He wanted to change the hidebound, bureaucratic, mutual organisation of one of Australia's oldest business insurance icons into an aggressive, flexible, growth-oriented public company. In the second year of his reign, he introduced six "AMP Shared Values", such as customer focus, teamwork and integrity, which he wanted to become the basis of a new corporate culture he was determined to implement.

He had the staff swear allegiance to nine "behaviour commitments" which were designed to reinforce the values he espoused. As on outsider and because of his very direct and confrontational style, he had his work cut out. Scepticism of what he was trying to do and how he was trying to do it undermined his efforts. But by dint of persistence and unwavering belief in what he was doing, he did succeed.

One person who was there said, 'People really got swept up in it, even those of us who were sceptics raised our hands. After that day the culture became one where even if you didn't believe in the AMP values, you had to behave as if you did because your bonus could depend on it." (*The Australian Financial Review*, 14-15 October 2000).

Despite the criticisms of Trumbull, he did manage to effect significant change internally in the AMP. Another CEO who axed the executive dining room, he nevertheless was able to relate to everyone in the organisation (except the Board) and gave the staff a feeling that they had his confidence. Perhaps it was his iconoclastic approach which soured his relations with the board and managed to offend everyone from shareholders to John Howard (at a prime ministerial dinner) that worked to his benefit with the staff.

Part of his assignment had been to break down the bureaucratic culture that had existed and in this he had largely succeeded. Perhaps he had come to the end of the line as an agent of change and did not have the personality which would allow a chameleon-like change to a more acceptable style.

"Everyone felt they had George's confidence. He got inside their heads and inspired them. That got the company a long way very quickly." (*The Australian Financial Review*, 14-15 October, 2000)

### ABC

Jonathan Shier, the managing director of the ABC appointed in 2000, appeared to have only one tool of change: fear. In his first eight months he removed most of the senior executives and replaced them with outside appointments. He replaced more than a dozen senior executives, including seven of the 12 ABC divisional heads. There is no doubt that in this process ABC lost some very talented people.

Shier's style was seen to be extremely remote and secretive. During these massive restructurings he apparently failed to communicate his vision of ABC's future to staff. His only address to the staff was an hour-long presentation with flow charts and graphic displays. This created a situation of utter confusion and distrust, as evidenced by the comments of staff and protest meetings.

Apart from being secretive, Shier appeared to quite deliberately distance himself from the staff. In August 2000, Robin Williams, an institution at ABC, hosted a party to celebrate the 25th anniversary of *The Science Show*. Several past executives showed up, but Shier did not.

Honouring the heroes is an essential part of the culture of an organisation, and the leader needs to be seen to be a part of that. Ian Henschke, the staff-elected director on the ABC board, says the regular bloodletting that occurred in the upper echelons of ABC could be enough to stop talented people from applying for senior positions. "It certainly sends the message to people below that there is an element of danger involved in the role. That could be enough for them to decide that it is not worth the risk, that there is a limited life in senior positions." (*The Australian Financial Review*, 14 October 2000) Shier did not last. He left after less than two years.

There is no doubt that firing staff can be an effective method of implementing change and sending a message to employees about acceptable behaviour and performance levels, but CEOs need to be careful that the process is seen as strategic and not random, or based just on personalities, otherwise it will just serve to make everybody keep their head down out of harm's way. It certainly will not help productivity.

## BHP

A very different culture change was evident following the appointment of another American CEO to what had been Australia's largest public company—BHP Ltd. Paul Anderson, brought in as CEO to BHP in December 1998 to try and restore value to a company that had suffered massive losses (some $13 billion in losses and write-offs over four years) and obviously needed some radical surgery, was the first outsider in its 115-year history.

He also removed a large proportion of senior executives, but in a way that was clearly associated with a major strategic restructuring. He implanted processes that made decision-making much more transparent, replacing what had been a culture of fear of making a recommendation that might incur the displeasure of top management.

He did this at the same time as making cultural changes that were insignificant in themselves, but massive in their impact. He introduced a casual style of dress (open necked shirts, no ties, no jackets) in a company where senior executives used to put on their suit coats (just jackets were not acceptable) before going to a meeting with top management. He preferred to dine in the staff cafeteria rather than the executive dining room, he abolished the hierarchy of company cars (as I did in one large public company when I was appointed CEO), and generally introduced an air of informality where staff felt more comfortable about approaching the CEO and top management and sharing ideas.

But he did this alongside implementing at the same time much more rigorous evaluation and assessment processes for major projects to avoid the sort of disastrous decisions that had been made under the previous regime. The casual dress code broke down barriers that were non-productive and helped to replace a culture that was conservative, rigid and inefficient with one that was more effective, efficient and flexible. It undoubtedly helped to energise people. Anderson was confident that there is no danger of staff confusing casual clothing with casual work practices. He believed you can make difficult and complex decisions without a tie.

All of these leaders have their own styles ranging from charismatic to quiet achievers, but they all had a firm belief in what needed to be done, their ability to do it, and were able to cope with a high degree of discomfort, unpleasantness and ambiguity. Leaders love ambiguity.

## Virgin Blue

One of the distinguishing features of Virgin Blue, the cut-price (low fare) airline launched in Australia in 2000 by Richard Branson, was a corporate culture distinctly different from its competitors. Its profile, its advertising, its operational procedures, even its language, projected a very different image compared to other airlines.

Brett Godfrey the founding CEO, says, "I feel our most unique 'selling points' differentials are our people and our culture… I think it is really important to develop a culture and nurture it long term and that's something that is difficult to do unless you start from scratch and build up… Virgin culture is unique worldwide and in Australia, our team, I believe, is more Virgin than Virgin… Our airline is different to any other company I have ever known. **The team culture is our only long-term competitive advantage.**" (my emphasis)

## **BOND University, School of Business**

On a somewhat different plane, when I became Dean of the School of Business at Bond University, Australia's first private university, I wanted to instill an appropriate culture in the students in the school. I introduced a Code of Honour. This was a very simple Code.

*As a Student at Bond University I pledge to abide by this Student Code of Honour.*

1.  *I shall at all times help and support my fellow students to derive full benefit from their time at the University.*
2.  *I shall honour the integrity, privacy and reputation of my fellow students and staff.*
3.  *I shall respect intellectual and physical property and will not use such property without the owner's permission.*
4.  *If I cheat, or if I have proof of another student cheating, and I fail to report this, I shall leave.*
5.  *If I plagiarise, or if I knowingly present another's work as my own or if I knowingly allow my own work to be presented as another's, I shall leave.*
6.  *I shall at all times support the development of the University as a centre of educational excellence.*
    *I hereby affirm that I have read and understood the provisions of the School of Business Code of Honour and agree to comply with the provisions of that Code."*

As Dean, I asked students to sign this Code on a purely voluntary basis. There was absolutely no compunction, no record of who signed or who did not. It was solely meant to signal what I felt were desirable and appropriate values for a university. As with all good codes, compliance was a matter of personal knowledge and behaviour, not one imposed by an external entity. I was not surprised when the practice ceased after I left the university.

At the Federal Council meeting of the Liberal Party in June 2005 in Canberra, Dr. Brendan Nelson, Minister for Education, Science and Training, outlined one of his projects: to introduce values into school curricula. I subsequently wrote to him to congratulate him and told him of my Code of Honour. He responded and agreed that there needed to be considerably more emphasis on values and ethics as part of any participation in higher education, and that a Code of Honour approach could be effective in addressing some of the root causes of cheating and plagiarism.

Much to my surprise and delight, he advised that he had written to the President of the Australian Vice-Chancellors Committee (AVCC), asking that the organisation consider whether there could be merit in adopting such an approach and whether it would be possible to obtain agreement on a code that could be adopted by all universities in Australia.

Again, I was not surprised when the AVCC decided to leave the matter to the discretion of individual universities. I am not holding my breath awaiting mass implementation.

## Time of Change

Leaders must have a total belief in their vision for the company, even when those around them might think they are crazy. They have to be prepared to accept that maybe nobody likes them. They have to be prepared to be disliked or unpopular (but not disrespected) for long periods of time. Many people cannot accept that and hence fail the test; their need to be liked is too strong.

What has to be recognised is that with the burning platform of change, at some point in time the fire has to be extinguished and replaced with a life raft of commitment and support from staff to the changes that have, and are, taking place.

Whilst it may take a long time to change a culture, unless significant change starts to take place within  months, or perhaps even weeks, morale will start to suffer, as people see no effect of the strains they are being put under, and cynicism starts to raise its non-productive head. Focus has to be redirected to the mission of the company and not the change process itself. This is an important point. During the change process there is a danger that the company may lose sight of its real purpose and take its eye off the ball. Managers and staff can become so absorbed in the change process that it becomes an end in itself instead of a means to an end. It is a very challenging period, because the company has to first survive to be a better company tomorrow. It serves little purpose to be the best organised, most efficient, bankrupt company.

One personal experience I had was chairing a company which, without any prior warning from management, or to be more honest, deliberately misleading the board, suffered a large loss in one year. At the first board meeting after becoming aware of the situation I sacked the senior management and installed myself (with the support of the board) as CEO as well as Chairman. In the three years following we made a profit every month (including the first month after the change).

The point is it was the same organisation, the same staff, the same products, the same competitors, and the same market. What was different was that we instilled a new culture- a culture of success. Staff were challenged to produce results and were rewarded accordingly. At the beginning there were many skeptics and doubters, but as the months rolled by without a loss, the company took on a new look. The impact of culture cannot be underestimated- but it has to come from the top.

When acquisitions/mergers fail, which is generally more than half, the reason often given is the different "cultures". Interestingly however, "culture" is rarely mentioned prior to the takeover or merger. An exception is Procter & Gamble, whose merger with Gillette recognised that the two companies had similar cultures and complementary core strengths in branding, innovation, scale and go-to-market capabilities.

Peter Drucker has observed that it is doubtful if culture can ever be "changed" and wrote that changing behaviour works only if it can be based on the existing "culture". He cites Konrad Adenauer, Germany's leader after World War II, as an example who understood this problem. In the 1920's, Adenauer was a vocal critic of Weimar Germany, yet, despite his aversion, he used the Weimar model to rebuild Germany, because it was the only culture Germans alive knew that still worked.

It is a mistake, however, to think of cultural change as something that happens at a point in time. It is continuous and must become part of everyone's job. Change is a constant and with the spread of technology, globalisation, and increased competition, the ability to manage change effectively is becoming a critical part of business leadership.

Globilisation has added another dimension of difficulty in that managing across differing national cultures, which may involve language, social, and religious differences is an added challenge. What needs to be remembered, however, is that there are some constants in business irrespective of culture- honesty, integrity and ethics. Without these no business will survive in the long run.

# CHAPTER 10 -

# Strategic I.Q.

*Failure is a better teacher than success.*

## A Popular Myth

Strategy plays a large part in a leader's life. Determining what business you are in, or what business you want to be in, or what business you have to be in, is the *sine qua non* of ultimate success and survival.

One of the most useful questions you can ask in business is whether you would enter the business if you were not already in it. Staying in a business is a much easier option than entering, and hence is a question too often avoided and even more often incorrectly answered.

It is up to leaders to set the direction of the business. Then their task is to get everybody else committed to and moving in the same direction. But determining the overall strategy for the business is a fundamental prerequisite. Libraries, particularly at management schools, have been filled with texts on strategy, strategic planning, and strategic management, most of which is theoretical nonsense, which in academic terms means practical nonsense as well. Unfortunately, we have hundreds of thousands of graduates who have been taught that it is the way to go.

Let me make myself very clear. I am not opposed to strategy. In the dictionary definition as a "plan of action or policy in business" it is a must in business. You have to have a plan of action. Clearly a business wandering along aimlessly is not going to last long. I am, therefore, strongly in favour of the outcome of strategy. What I am vigorously opposed to is the process by which so-called strategy is developed—the furphy of strategic planning.

The idea of all the senior executives getting together once a year in a so-called "retreat" (when it should be called an "advance") to devise the future strategy for the business, documenting what is going to happen, setting goals (generally based on past performance) for the next three years, and ending up with a Strategic Plan signed off by the CEO and subsequently endorsed by the Board that is of any practical value, is sheer fantasy.

The spectre of thousands of strategic plans in nicely labeled and indexed three-ring binders sitting on executive bookshelves conjures up the feast a poltergeist would have in exorcising the devilish instruments.

Sanford "Sandy" Weill became an American business legend as Chairman and CEO of Citigroup in the late 1990's. He became a legend in the financial services world. In her biography of Weill, Monica Langley (Langley, p.121) told a story of when Weill had taken over Commercial Credit Corporation, an unsuccessful subsidiary of Control Data, a computer manufacturer. At his first staff meeting he was asked by the head of the strategic planning department, "Sandy, can you share with us your philosophy of strategic planning?" Weill replied, "I get up in the morning, I read the *Wall Street Journal*, and I make a strategic plan for the day." The department head looked stricken. This was someone who created massive books of five-year plans, and it was painfully clear the new boss would have no use for all those plans. Citigroup continued to go from strength to strength and became the world's largest financial services company while Sandy Weill was still chairman. (Recent history in the global financial crisis of 2008 has not been as kind-for a whole host of diverse reasons).

One of the problems with the traditional approach is that best practice says you have to have measurable goals and milestones. You need to be able to measure your progress against the stated goals. You have to be able to gauge whether or not you are making progress.

The problem for the visionary leader with this approach is that in trying to crystallise the big vision, often the quantification gives free reign to the skeptics to destroy the idea. Remember that the natural reaction is to resist change. There will be many more out there who want the idea to fail rather than succeed. Giving them the opportunity to illustrate the foolishness of the idea by showing just how difficult it is to quantify the progress of the idea is providing succor to the enemy.

Another of the great dangers of the traditional approach with its emphasis on forecasting and budgets is that they are invariably based on the past. This is probably the worst way to try and predict the future. Budgets are invariably conservative, risk averse, and easily achievable. They also generally are completely inward looking.

One of the most unreliable indicators of the future is the past. Businesses continually make the mistake of building their future on the past. How often do you see budgets prepared on the basis of "x%" above last year as the target? One thing this approach does is completely ignore competitors and the market. It is making decisions in a vacuum. Not good.

What we should do is work backwards not forwards. We should be setting our goals on what we want to achieve in three or five years, and working back to see what has to be done to achieve those outcomes. One result is generally a severe shock at the size of the task ahead. Good leaders go about the task of doing what has to be done. They accept the challenge. Poor leaders will immediately question the "feasibility", the "practicality", the "wisdom", and the "financial viability" of the goals and set about making them "more realistic". This is why Strategic IQ is so important.

Budgeting is inevitably a lowest common denominator or minimisation approach. This achieves the best results down the track when actuals are compared with budget. They set future targets on the basis of what has been achieved in the past, when the real task is to set targets that beat the hell out of the opposition. Increasing our performance by 30% on last year and telling ourselves how well we are doing is of little consequence if our competition is growing at 100% and our business is declining as a result.

Strategy is often confused with vision. They are two completely different things. Vision is the beacon on the hill, the picture of what the business is going to be, written large on the tapestry of the future. It is the "what" issue. Strategy is all about the way in which the vision is going to be achieved. It is the How issue.

## Strategic IQ

The most successful companies do not try to constrain initiative by making all segments of the business fit into some sort of central overall organisational plan. What successful strategy is all about is not a central strategic plan, but a central idea and the organisational culture to build on that idea at every opportunity. This is what I call "Strategic IQ".

Strategic IQ is about getting a business to clearly understand the vision ; to absorb it into the pores via osmosis so that everyone in the business knows without the shadow of a doubt WHAT the business is about.

When we talk about "the business" we really mean "the people in the business". So, Strategic IQ is imbuing in everybody in the business a clear, unambiguous and common understanding of the goals and aspirations of the business.

To use the GE example. Everybody in GE knows that unless they are ranked one or two in that business in the world marketplace, they will not last as part of GE. In the same vein, Welch believed that GE was too big and diverse to have a strategy per se, as he noted in his first major speech some 20 years ago (presciently entitled "Growing Fast in a Slow-Growth Economy"). It had a set of ideas and initiatives which the CEO promoted throughout the company's 12 businesses.

Welch had four major thrusts: globalisation, services, digitization, and the quality program known as Six Sigma. These ideas or goals were unceasingly promoted throughout the whole organisation. There was no doubt in anybody's mind as to what was seen to be important. Executives had a very clear framework in which to plan their businesses. They had a very clear view of what they needed to do to succeed in GE.

Consequently, when opportunities arose they could decide very quickly if they fitted GE. They could focus on those opportunities which satisfied the initiatives that Welch constantly articulated. This is what I call Strategic IQ. They "knew" whether it was an opportunity they should pursue or not. It did not have to have been foreseen in some strategic planning session and incorporated in some voluminous tome signed off by the omnipotent CEO and the even wiser Board of Directors. No. It either fitted the direction GE was headed or it did not.

An executive team with clearly focused Strategic IQ is much better prepared to recognise opportunities as they present themselves, because they see them through a different prism. They do not see them as "businesses" which had been identified or targeted as acquisitions, or "markets" which had been targeted as "new opportunities". They saw the opportunity as one which matched the "ideas" they were pursuing.

Business is constantly changing. There are so many facets impacting on business that cannot be predicted. The external environment be it social, economic, financial, political, or religious is completely unpredictable. It is foolish to pretend that we can predict the situation three years down the track, or even one year. The global financial crisis of 2008 is a perfect example of this. How then can we have precise plans as to what we intend to do? The answer is: we cannot.

How then do we cope with the future? We cannot just wring our hands and say it is all too hard. If we realise that we have to deal with continually changing circumstances we can then appreciate that strategy is all about the evolution of a central idea through those continually changing circumstances. The future is impossible to anticipate by detailed planning, but it is possible to hold an idea and place it into different circumstances. This is what strategy is really about. And leaders build organisations that are adept at making ideas work in ever-changing environments—by developing Strategic IQ.

The great danger of a detailed plan is that unexpected events will destroy the plan. Unexpected events cannot destroy a great idea. Strategy is the evolution of the idea through changing circumstances. The challenge, particularly in large companies, is to create an environment where people can achieve their dreams, and they do not have to do it in their garage or on the kitchen table.

Inertia, the lethargy of mass, is the obstacle that leaders have to expunge from large organisations so that they operate like small organisations. Businesses like ABB (Asea Brown Boveri) do this by breaking the company up worldwide into small operating groups with significant autonomy. Each of these groups has a very clear understanding of the business they are in and the vision of ABB. They have a clear set of goals and they grasp every opportunity that presents itself, because they have Strategic IQ.

The secret is to use the benefits of size, the financial, technological, market, and educational benefits of a large organisation and marry them to the lack of bureaucracy, speed of response, decisiveness, and agility of a small organisation. There is a credo in football that the good big player will always beat the good little player. Similarly, in business being big and agile is better than being little and agile.

Strategic IQ is about not being surprised by being surprised in the future. Those organisations which have not developed Strategic IQ, but have relied on old-fashioned strategic planning are generally surprised, not prepared for the surprise, and resistant to change.

Under Sandy Weill, Citigroup, and the other companies he led, are a good example of Strategic IQ. Sandy had monthly "planning group" meetings. He and his senior executives would assemble after breakfast in comfortable, overstuffed armchairs and he would open the meeting with his signature line: "Let's talk deals."

On a white board, one of his executives would then write column headings such as "insurance" and "securities". The other executives would then call out names of possible merger candidates. Within a few minutes the board would be filled with the names of potential takeover targets. Then they would discuss the possibilities and come to a conclusion. Perhaps none of them would be pursued. Perhaps one or more would be. But they were all well aware of where they wanted to go and were constantly identifying potential targets. And they did not have a five volume planning manual to guide them. In fact, one of Weill's proud boasts was that he did not read memos. And in a remarkable and successful career that was how he operated, and Citigroup became one of the biggest banks in the world.

Somewhat closer to home we have a similar example. In 2004, Bruce Mathieson made a joint bid with Woolworths for the pubs and pokies group Australian Leisure & Hospitality (ALH) at a price of $1.3 billion. Mathieson has amassed a personal fortune of some $400 million. The group has a portfolio of 135 hotels in five states, 5981 gaming machines across four states and 266 retail liquor outlets.

Mathieson has one mantra: Keep it Simple. He is reported (Business Review Weekly,4-10 August, 2005) as saying, "All the major decisions you make in your life, such as getting married, it's all done by gut instinct. But when we go to make a business decision we want a piece of paper. It just doesn't make sense to me."

His business philosophy is guaranteed to give Deans of Business Schools high blood pressure. "Business is basically very simple to me because I am not educated. Most people you deal with are educated so they are automatically complicated. I've never written a letter in my life, never looked at a computer and never had a secretary. It's the best thing that ever happened to me." He adds, "The cheapest thing in the world to buy is brains. You can buy brains anywhere."

Bruce Mathieson's vast knowledge of the industry, his 30 years experience in the game, his intelligence, his vision, his gut instinct as he calls it, are what I call Strategic IQ. He has it in spades and organisations, if they want to be successful, should develop it.

Woolworth's CEO, Roger Corbett, was undoubtedly a proponent of Strategic IQ. He presided over a very successful seven years as CEO before retiring in late 2006. When asked about some of the major acquisitions and other strategic decisions during his term, he said (*The Australian Financial Review*, 27 February 2006, p.13), "What happened is that the opportunities came along. They were commercial opportunities we had scoped and had on our radar. When circumstances converged we moved. We'd been managing our balance sheet and resources to be able to fully take advantage of these opportunities."

Strategic IQ is not about trying to foretell the future and following a carefully laid out plan ; it is about being ready to move quickly when opportunities arise. Interestingly, politics is a much more fertile ground for the application of Strategic IQ than business. Politics is all about grand plans and visions.

John Howard, as Prime Minister of Australia from 1996-2007, was an outstanding leader. He had a very clear idea of what he wanted to achieve and had no fear in articulating his vision. He did not do this by having weekend "strategy retreats". He did not do it by producing multi-volume "strategic plans". He did it by having a very clear idea of the sort of Australia he believed Australians wanted, and by having a central idea on what would deliver the necessary outcomes. He then made sure that ministers and others had a clear and unequivocal understanding of the desired outcomes.

In other words, he positioned the government so that it could take advantage of whatever situation developed that accorded with the desired outcomes; his immediate response to the Port Arthur murders was the enactment of stronger gun laws; his implementation of a Goods and Services Tax, despite having previously said his government would not introduce one ; his pursuit of industrial reform for over 20 years (with perhaps in hindsight a liitle too much aggression); his focus on family values.

It was this focus on a clearly defined set of principles that led to the oft quoted observation that "Everyone knows what John Howard stands for." It is an observation that does not apply to a lot of other political leaders.

As stated above, "What successful strategy is all about is not a central strategic plan but a central idea and the organisational culture to build on that idea at every opportunity." This is precisely what Howard did so successfully with the Liberal-led government.

Leadership is about initiating change, and hence developing Strategic IQ is an essential part of preparing an organisation to be ready to cope with change. If change is seen as a threat, as something to be feared and resisted, the result is failure.

If change is welcomed as opening up new opportunities, of presenting new challenges, which of themselves offer the chance to increase benefits and rewards, then success will follow. Citigroup is a great example of this.

In the following chapter we shall be discussing change in more detail.

## Decision-making

Decision-making, and the nature of decisions, are important ingredients in building Strategic IQ. The nature of the decision-making in an organisation communicates to those in the organisation not only directions in which the organisation is moving, but also some of the ways in which it is moving. In other words, decisions give a clue not only to the Whats, but also the Hows.

It was in my undergraduate years (1959) in studying Public Administration that I came across *Administrative Behavior* by Herbert Simon, first published in 1945. I became an ardent fan of Simon and read everything he wrote over succeeding decades. I still have the 1957 edition on my bookshelves, along with many of the successive publications, both by himself and with March, Newell and others.

In later years I was drawn back to his notion of "intelligence-design-choice" sequence in decision-making (Simon, 1960, p.2). "Intelligence" refers to the data and information relevant to the problem collected by the decision maker. "Design" is the formulation of options or solutions for the matter in hand. "Choice" then refers to the selection amongst those solutions of the one that the decision-maker is going to apply. Along with his concept of "bounded rationality", it provides an elegant foundation for Strategic IQ.

Simon (1957, p.75) defines rationality, "...concerned with the selection of preferred behavior alternatives in terms of some system of values whereby the consequences of behavior can be evaluated." He noted that this might be conscious or unconscious behaviour.

However, decisions in organisations are the result of information coming from a variety of sources both within and without the organisation. Whilst Simon is at one end of the spectrum, another model was developed at the other end of the spectrum to cater for this fact. In this model (e.g. Hickson et al, 1986) we see decisions emerging, with no apparent structure or sequence, from a mass of unstructured data and information.

There were those who were still dissatisfied with the models and saw somewhere near the mid-point of the spectrum a process which combined elements of both the foregoing. Mintzberg et al (1976) took the linear sequence of the Simon model and then imposed a series of interruptions and interventions that reflected the more chaotic nature of the second model. In this model the decision-maker begins with something tangible e.g. a problem to be solved, and whilst trying to stay focused and "on-track", is inevitably sidetracked by the real world of unpredictability, conflict and intervention. This gives us a third model.

Strategic IQ recognizes that A decision is often many decisions taken over a period of time, and often without any realisation that they bear any relationship to one another or to a pending decision. This introduces the idea of "convergence" (model four) in the decision process and it is a key factor in Strategic IQ. The emergence of a new model automobile is not the result of A decision. It is the outcome of probably thousands of separate decisions. The success of the new model will depend on how well those decisions "converge" on the core values and goals of the organisation.

Leadership involves building decision-making and decision-making processes in ways that optimise this convergence. Hage (1980) and others have pursued this approach. The missing ingredient in all of these approaches is a recognition that the decision-maker is a human being. Decision-making is not just a process, it is behaviour. In his *New Science of Management Decisions,* (Simon, 1977), identified the role "judgement, intuition, and creativity" play in decision-making. He elaborated on this in later writings (1987) in which he emphasised the importance to the exercise of intuition of the way in which knowledge was organised.

It is this human intuitive creativity that transforms the IQ into Strategic. It is the recognition and realisation that this needs to be nurtured that brings leadership to the fore. Leaders, as opposed to shepherds, entrepreneurs or managers, know that to replicate the drive, inspiration, and creativity needed at all levels of the organisation that Strategic IQ is a necessary pre-requisite.

Therefore, Strategic IQ has to supply a framework in which these human attributes will be channeled to produce complementary outcomes and not conflicting outcomes. Strategic IQ has to have a framework of inspiration within which decisions are taken. Inspiration lies at the heart of leadership, and therefore Strategic IQ tends to correlate with effective leadership. But the important contribution of the decision-making process to the building of Strategic IQ is not just in the process, but also in the nature of the decisions themselves. I categorise decisions as being inspirational, satisficing (just enough to satisfy), challenging or routine. These typologies match the mobilisation categories I outlined earlier.

Leaders tend to make inspirational decisions. The decisions themselves reflect the nature of the leadership. Decisions that set seemingly impossible goals tend to enthuse, inspire and motivate those who have to carry them out.

Shepherds, on the other hand, tend to make decisions that help to maintain the status quo without any major disruption or intervention. Entrepreneurs, by their very nature, are thrusting into new areas and their decisions throw out further challenges to be overcome on the road to success. Managers are interested in maintaining good order, and their decisions will therefore be routine in terms of options that are available.

## Genius of the AND

In helping to build convergence and extending the number of options available, the notion of the AND promoted by Collins and Porras is a very valuable strategic concept. They compare what they call "the Genius of the AND" with the "Tyranny of the OR" and make the very valid point that too often we focus on one thing to the exclusion of the other.

For example:
You can have change OR stability.
You can be conservative OR bold.
You can have low cost OR high quality.
You can invest for the future OR do well in the short term
    and of particular relevance to this discussion.
You can make progress by methodical planning OR by opportunistic groping.

Clearly, forcing a choice between seemingly competing or contradictory alternatives is a severe constraint on the number of options that might be considered in formulating a future strategy. This is in direct contrast to the idea of Strategic IQ whereby the culture in the organisation is deliberately built around the constant, willing and proactive seeking of potential strategic options.

Think of the opportunities that are created by replacing the OR with an AND. We suddenly have a whole new set of challenges. It is possible to have BOTH low cost and high quality, and the business that achieves that has a significant competitive advantage. It might be argued that it is just too difficult to try to pursue conflicting goals at the same time. This is probably true, but it should not defeat the opportunity to achieve desirable outcomes. How much better to be able to deliver on both fronts.

F. Scott Fitzgerald pointed out, "The test of a first-rate intelligence is the ability to hold two opposed ideas in the mind at the same time, and still retain the ability to function."

Visionary companies need to do the same—with Strategic IQ.

(Postscript- I drafted this chapter some three years ago and I was both bemused and reassured to read a headline in *The Australian Financial Review* of 30 December 2008 (pp.24-25), "The Strategy Fad Is Dead, Long Live Thinking".

The article traversed the work of Porter, and the criticisms of Hamel and Mintzberg, and the work of Tapscott and Kotter. Marc Stigter, the program director of the advanced management program at Mt. Eliza Executive Education, part of the Melbourne Business School says, "I've always been skeptical about the concept of 'strategy' because I have been part of so many strategies that have failed. About eight out of 10 strategies fail and 80 per cent of companies are dissatisfied with their strategies."

The article suggests the answer may be concentrating on the how , which is exactly what I argue above.

Richard Rumelt, professor of business and society at the Anderson School of Management , University of California, makes the point that strategy is neither a document or a forecast but rather an overall approach based on a coherent viewpoint about the forces at work, not a plan.

As Stigter concludes, "Strategy is not about methodology and frameworks, it's a mindset or philosophy."

My sentiments exactly. What I call Strategic IQ.)

# CHAPTER 11 -

# Leading Change

*Without Change There is No Tomorrow*

## Leading Change

The essence of leadership is change. Leaders only exist to change things, be it a business, a religion, a political party, a government, a battle, a nation, or the world. The status quo is anathema to them. Without the need for change, leaders are a luxury we can do without. But it is this very focus on change which is important. We generally talk of *managing change* when we should be talking of *leading change*.

Change itself needs to be understood as a driver of the business. Change can be incremental or it can be massive. Incremental change is generally not worth the effort. If you have a Boeing 747 which transports 350 passengers at 900 kilometres per hour, designing one that carries 400 passengers at 1000 kilometres per hour is not particularly useful, compared with designing one that carries 700 people at 1500 kilometres per hour.

If a leader is to initiate change, it needs to be significantly different from the status quo. It has to jump start the future. It represents for the whole organisation a decisive break from the past. When radical change occurs in markets, competition, technology, and customers, responses that might have been adequate for incremental change are no longer adequate for radical change. Organisations and the people in them have to adapt to what might be almost unknown territory. Leaders have to mobilise people to accept that adaptation, to accept new processes, new products, new structures, new strategies, new behaviours, and new ways of thinking. Not just different, but new.

In leading change, leaders have to manage the rate of change. "Manage" does not mean, as it is probably assumed at first blush, "slow down" or "reduce". Change, if it is to be meaningful, has to be what I call "threshold change".

## Threshold Change

It has to be of such magnitude and so much different from the status quo that there is absolutely no doubt in anybody's mind that big things are underway. It has to be so different that it forces people to consider new ways of thinking and doing things. But on the other hand, it has to be seen to be believable and achievable.

Hence, threshold change takes people to the edge of the current system and shows them the other side of the divide. But they can see the other side and know it is real. They know it is going to take superhuman efforts to make the other side, but it is doable. And the rewards will be worth it. That is threshold change.

When I joined the insurance company I was recruited to put some order into the chaos of the computer systems. The company was six months behind in issuing renewal notices. For an insurance company this is fatal unless corrected quickly. It was also about to commission a new computer system, which was likely to exacerbate the whole problem.

One of their major projects was to bring together all the business of a client. Today this would be called CRM (Customer Relationship Management). In 1970 we did not have a name for it. And in 1970 it was a major undertaking. A decision had been taken to do this by giving each customer a unique number and linking all their business to that number—policies, claims and so on. This is what I call a management decision.

One of my first actions was to stop this approach and direct (not consult and consensus) that another unique identifier would be used –the individual's name, which most people find easier to remember than a 16-digit number.

There was an immediate plethora of arguments put forward as to why this was (with the hardware and software then available) neither feasible, logical, nor even sensible. This approach was also to incorporate going on-line (with the first set of terminals the company had ever had—it was leading edge technology) and real-time. The cost was in the millions. This was threshold change. It was achieved on time and for the next 20 years that insurance company was a leader in its field in the application of information technology.

In an increasingly competitive and global world it is likely that there will be more radical change rather than less. Strategic IQ becomes more important because radical change can only be satisfactorily handled by everybody in the organisation adapting. At all levels, and in every part of the organisation, new solutions have to be found. The organisation in total has to adapt and the collective intelligence, the Strategic IQ, is the mechanism by which this is done.

The other side of the coin is the "unlearning" that is necessary. The discarding of inappropriate behaviour, processes, and ways of thinking will only occur if leaders constantly challenge people at all levels to themselves challenge the "way we do business". In this process, competing values and norms have to be resolved.

## Creative Conflict

In these sorts of circumstances there tends to be lots of conflict. People react differently to radical change and it is inevitable that in finding the most appropriate response there will be a variety of experiments tried. Some will work, some will not.

This becomes a critical time for leaders. If the conflict gets out of hand, performance obviously suffers. Leaders have to manage this conflict. This does not necessarily mean eliminating or eradicating all conflict. Apart from it being completely unrealistic to think it is possible to have nothing but sweetness and light, a little conflict is a good thing.

Conflict, if properly managed, can be productive. A little "creative conflict" can generate useful ideas and positive momentum. People at different levels have different knowledge which they bring to bear on the new changed circumstances. This will inevitably generate some opposing thoughts on what and how things should be done.

## Core Values

Whilst change is what leaders feed on, one aspect of most successful companies which does not undergo constant change is its core ideology. In some of the most successful companies, core values have remained intact for decades. Change and adaptation can occur without scrapping the core values.

Whilst core values may remain, oftentimes there is a need to transform the underlying culture of the organisation. How people behave in an organisation in a given set of circumstances is determined by the culture of the organisation. Culture legitimises certain forms of action and proscribes other forms.

For example, one of the core values may be to deliver quality products, but the culture may be to do this without regard to costs. The challenge is to retain the core value, but change the culture.

Culture is a very amorphous creature and leaders need to be sensitive to its vagaries. The organisation will have its culture, there may well be "role" cultures related to specific jobs in the organisation, professional groups such as accountants, engineers, lawyers and so on will have their own culture, and all of these need to be taken into account. In an increasingly multicultural society, care needs to be exercised in respect of race, religion, and other ethnic aspects.

Leaders need to realise that changing culture, or for that matter implanting a culture in a new organisation, is a lengthy and time-consuming task. It cannot be done overnight, and it cannot be turned on and off. Difficult though it may be, leaders ignore culture at their peril. Change can be torpedoed by an inappropriate culture. An essential prerequisite is for the leader to understand the existing culture and the values it is based on.

Changing culture may also require changing organisational structures. This can often be an effective way for a leader to bring about change. It tends to break some of the historical links and relationships.

## It's Still People

At the outset I said leadership is all about people. Change is a very personal thing. Leaders have to win their followers over one by one. It cannot be done in bulk. One of the difficulties for leaders is that change is often the most foreign task they have to undertake. They may have all the expertise and technical skills in the world, but leading change can be a whole new experience. What makes change a complex operation is that it has so many facets, all of which have to be dealt with simultaneously.

One of the important things a leader must do in leading change is to make the process transparent. Everyone in the organisation should be fully informed at all times as to what is happening, the problems and how they are being solved, and the progress that is being made. An information vacuum is asking for trouble.

If people do not know what is happening, they will assume the worst and react accordingly. Usually the rumours are much worse than what is really happening. Change invariably meets unforeseen obstacles. Leaders should take the opportunity to involve followers in resolving these barriers. This gives everybody a sense of ownership and hence a stronger commitment to make it work.

Leaders often make the mistake of thinking that everyone in the organisation is as mad keen on the changes as they are. This is almost universally not the case. Leaders need to avoid the danger of over-optimism and over-confidence. Leaders need to appreciate that you cannot legislate change. Change requires convincing. And convincing means seeing results. Change is an emotional thing. People's feelings are at stake. Change needs to capture the heart as well as the mind.

# CHAPTER 12 -

# Leadership in the 21st Century

*Always assume you're right, until someone proves you are.*

## Introduction

In the 21st century, things will be much as they are today, only more so. It is tempting to paint a scenario of tremendous change driven by all pervasive technologies (primarily, but not exclusively information, communication and bio-technologies) and globalisation, with manufacturing roboticised, distribution automated with GPS controlled deliveries, and b2b, b2c, c2c, etc., all electronic. One might then wonder what effect this will have on leadership.

It will have a significant effect on management, and management skills will need to be much more diverse than today. The traditional management functions of planning, controlling, organising and so on will still be much the same, but the context in which they are applied will be very different. The convergence of technologies in a constantly changing global market-place will create new demands on management, particularly in the area of information or knowledge management.

The impact on leadership will be less dramatic, but no less critical, and it will revolve around information and knowledge, particularly the differenti-ation of meaningful and relevant information from the exponentially mul-tiplying masses of irrelevant information. It is particularly important for Australia in this context. With the increasing globalisation of business, the advent of e-commerce, mega mergers, increased shareholder activity, and the continual redefining of business goals, strong business leadership is critical. And for Australia, with few companies straddling the globe, we face the danger of becoming a business backwater without the drive of dynamic leadership, not only in business, but also in government and research.

Globally, leaders will be operating in a world economy increasingly influenced by China and India as major powers, along with the USA,Japan and Asia.. The emergence of Eastern Europe from Communism, particularly Russia, will have a significant impact. Labour markets, as well as financial and product markets, will become global. This will require more sophisticated strategies, as leadership is about people. In the coming century the changes are likely to be more frequent, more rapid and more global (witness the global financial crisis of 2008). The opportunities for leadership are likely to increase, as are the challenges of leadership.

In the workplace of the future, the most important ingredients will be people and knowledge. The technologies which are mesmerising us today will be recognised for what they really are—the embedded tools for doing business. Australian business leaders will have (very) belatedly come to understand that it is the "I" which is important and not the "T". "Information" will be finally recognised as the key ingredient and "technology" merely as the delivery mechanism.

Just on 30 years ago I published an article in SEARCH, the Journal of the Australian and New Zealand Association for the Advancement of Science, entitled "Information as a Commodity", in which I emphasised the value of information as opposed to the technology.

A decade later another paper I wrote was titled "The Bifurcation of the IT Professional". Again I attempted to highlight the importance of the "I" in the IT equation and tried to warn IT professionals of the threats they were facing from other professions, especially engineering and accounting, which were increasingly tending to encroach more and more into the areas of activity hitherto regarded as the preserve of the IT professional.

In 1996, I published a paper in the *Australian Accountant* titled "The IT Professional: the I, the T or Neither?" Again I made the point, "IT managers and accountants are sitting on the most valuable resource of the organisation: information". I was making the point yet again that information was the important ingredient, and not the technology, although we almost invariably tended to focus most of our attention on the technology.

To date it has been just the opposite. The technology has been seen as the basis for competitive advantage rather than the knowledge it provides. The technologists have been in the ascendancy because of the inexcusable ignorance of senior management of the real value of the technology, which is its outputs.

Feeble attempts to recognise the changes taking place by creating new jobs with titles such as Chief Information Officer (CIO), only reinforce the lack of understanding of what is really happening. Such jobs are invariably more accurately described as Chief Information Technology Officer or Chief Information Systems Officer. One thing they are not is Chief Information Officer.

Similarly, the emphasis on information overload as one of the key problems of the future fails to recognize the failure of the technology. It is not the sheer volume of information, which is increasing exponentially, that creates the difficulty. It is the failure to develop technology-based knowledge interpreters that distill the knowledge we want (and perhaps need) from the morass of irrelevancy. I currently chair a fledgling IT company working in this space.

One of the most exciting developments will be the new ways of analysing, interpreting, synthesising, and presenting information and knowledge. There will be much more emphasis on visualisation and simulation. We will, at last, start tapping into the untapped power of the brain to digest information in visual form. The old Chinese proverb, "One picture is worth a thousand words" will finally be applied to the use of technology to improve our knowledge transformation.

It is nonsense to suggest that one of the key drivers of tomorrow's economy will be technology. Everybody will have it and if they do not use it, they will not survive. It will be a given. It will be knowledge that will provide sustainable competitive advantage and knowledge is the capital of people.

Let us look at the changes we are likely to see in the next century in the players in the leadership process and in the process itself.

## Changes for Leaders

In Australia, it is inevitable that women will emerge increasingly in leadership (except perhaps at some of the leading Men's Clubs). At the present they are one of our most underutilised resources. This has to change. And it will introduce some changes to the leadership we have been used to. Women often bring different attitudes, different skills, and a different set of values to leadership. I emphasise sometimes and different. There is no suggestion of better or worse.

In relation to the issue of women in leadership there are several strands of thought. One is that women, by their very gender, bring to their task qualities that men lack ; attributes such as collaboration, affiliation, intuition, and nurturing, all of which are particularly relevant to people relationships and hence leadership. Those who favour this line of thought argue that women tend to be more participatory in their leadership style and more caring of their followers. It is also claimed that women are better right-brain thinkers and hence more creative and flexible than men.

Like all generalisations there are exceptions, and the opponents of the foregoing view use these to support their line of argument that both sexes have a masculine and feminine side to their nature, which is reflected in their leadership style. What needs to be done is to create a climate in the organisation in which everyone feels free to express these characteristics.

Another point of view is that the converse proposition, that women are capable of exhibiting 'masculine' qualities, must also be true—"look like a lady; act like a man"—the 'she-male'. Margaret Thatcher is given as the supreme example.

An alternative view is that there is no evidence that male and female qualities exist. Be that as it may, in Australia we will see more women leaders emerge, and because of the changes we will see in followers, as discussed later, the sorts of characteristics described above as 'female' will of necessity become more important to effective leadership, irrespective of gender. We will see more "look like a lady, act like a lady" and more "look like a man, act like a lady". This is not to suggest an androgynous approach, but rather an appreciation of the differences. This will require people in power, who are mostly men, and who tend to promote people most like themselves, to 'open their minds' to the changes that are taking place.

As perception is a critical feature of leadership, the mere increase in the proportion of women in leadership roles will bring about significant change in the generally macho Australian context.

The networked world also offers the opportunity of gender-free and racially-free virtual communication, as opposed to face-to-face, which will provide a working environment with a greater focus on what is done rather than who might do it.

On the other hand, this environment will create a demand for new or enhanced skills in leaders. Negotiation and conflict resolution will take on new dimensions in a networked world. Think of the difficulties of trying to resolve in a virtual context conflicting demands of say employees in vastly different cultures and environments. There are many businesses today which operate in a diversity of environments, but the critical difference is the virtual nature of the context, and that makes an enormous difference.

The knowledge economy will undoubtedly generate not only new businesses but also new business models. These will be both economic models and organisational models. New models will require new forms of leadership. Kotter (2001) describes this as 5 Degrees of Change from businesses with little change, through continuous improvement, non-incremental change within businesses, whole new businesses, to whole new business models. He sees leadership moving from basic management for levels 1 and 2, through visionary leadership for level 3, and levels 4 and 5 requiring energy-unleashing leadership.

Energy-unleashing leadership taps deeply into people's hopes and dreams, most basic human values, and needs for a meaningful life. He sees energy-unleashing leaders more adept at role-modeling, and tapping deeper into the psyche than their predecessors to release greater passion and creative power to shape exceptionally bold group goals.

He sees "doing what is right" as the guiding principal, and it's created by appealing to very basic human values, by appealing to that which we share regardless of educational background, nationality, religion, or race: a desire for security for self and family, for love, for respect, for opportunities to grow, for a sense of purpose in one's life. The talk goes beyond what we do (strategies) or how we do things (rules) to who we are. What he is suggesting is that a very strong form of transformational leadership will be necessary for winning in the new economy.

His "tough new goals" smacks of the BHAGS (Big Hairy Audacious Goals) of Collins & Porras (1994). Huge daunting challenges like "this Nation should commit itself to achieving the goal, before this decade is out, of landing a man on the moon and returning him safely to earth." A BHAG is a clarion call to arms setting such a challenging goal that it gives leadership the opportunity of creating great enthusiasm and commitment, like Ford's "To democratise the automobile". This helped Ford emerge from the ruck of a number of then competing companies to become dominant in the industry.

For those (Goleman, 1995, 1998) who regard *emotional intelligence* as the *sine qua non* of leadership success, the next century is likely to place more emphasis on the attributes that make up that characteristic-self-awareness, self-regulation, motivation, empathy, and social skill. It is not hard to imagine Kotter's energy-unleashing leadership tapping into the human psyche, drawing more heavily on these components.

A critical factor for leaders will be not so much what they know as how quickly they can learn. Senge (1993) introduced us to the learning organisation. The five new "component technologies": systems thinking, personal mastery, mental models, building shared vision, and team learning, which in regard to human behaviour, he said should be seen as *disciplines*. There is no doubt these disciplines will be a central factor in organisational success in the current century.

It will be vital for leaders to be able to readily access the right information and demonstrate a high degree of flexibility and adaptability in dealing with both technology and people. In a networked world they will also need the ability to stay interconnected themselves.

Leadership skills will need to have much more depth. Communicating with stakeholders takes on a new dimension, as does seeking input from employees. Inspiring a team in Australia is not the same challenge as inspiring a team made up of Australians, Japanese, and Russians. The hard-nosed, top-down directive must be replaced with a more flexible, empathetic approach, still keeping to the core values of the organisation and the goals established.

Visions, so essential to effective leadership and inspiring the troops, will require great skill in their creation and articulation to a group of diverse interests, backgrounds, and situations, the latter being the prime differentiator between today and tomorrow.

Leaders in Australia will eventually appreciate the importance of language skills, not just because of their communication benefits, but because of their importance in understanding other cultures. Kevin Rudd, the current prime minister, a fluent speaker of Mandarin, is a relevant example.

As leadership is essentially about creating change, the new economy will require much more sensitivity to the change process. In the past we have seen on the one hand the emphasis on economic value in the change process—the Dunlap approach for example, which we have witnessed in Australia. This involves drastic staff reductions, downsizing, closing businesses and generally focusing on the bottom line. On the other hand we have the approach which concentrates on changing organisational capacity. This concentrates on corporate culture: employee behaviours, attitudes, capabilities and commitment (Beer and Nohria, 2000).

Leaders in the next century will have to combine these approaches rather than seeing them as alternatives. (Refer to the Genius of the AND earlier). Failure to do this will not generate the level of radical change needed to transform businesses in the networked world.

## Changes for Followers

Followers will be better educated and will have a greater diversity of backgrounds. There are too many capable people leaving Australia and seeking greener pastures overseas. There are a number of reasons for this, but it is having a debilitating effect not only on business, but also in our universities, where it is becoming increasingly difficult to retain and attract quality staff. One of the saddest aspects of very recent years in this country has been the dramatic decline in the field of tertiary education, when Australia is compared to the rest of the world. It will require very strong leadership in the 21st century to reverse this decline and lift our **investment** in education to the point where we are globally competitive **with the best in the world.**

As probably 50% of the jobs that will exist in the 21st century have not yet been thought of, it is rather difficult to define the specifics, but we do know that the majority of the new occupations will be knowledge based. It has been suggested (*Business Review Weekly*, 24 November, 2000, p.64), that we will see titles such as Director of Intellectual Capital, Data Mining Officer, Chief Futurist, Talent Manager, Retention Manager, Chief Evangelist, Manager for Diversity, Director of People, and so on. It is predicted that in 10 years no one will be called an accountant, but will be a resource allocation adviser.

Whilst we may read these sorts of predictions with a jaundiced eye, just thinking of the jobs that exist today that did not exist even 50 years ago puts the scenario into reality. We already have (*Business Review Weekly*, 24 November, 2000, p.65) Chief Growth Officer, Creatologist, Culture Team Leader, Messaging Champion, and Apostle of Partners. I saw an application recently with the title of Chief Visionary—he had created the company some years before.

KPMG had a Chief Knowledge Officer as had the Australian Taxation Office. The following ad appeared in the *The Australian Financial Review* on 1 May 1998. "Chief Knowledge Director"—"harness, guide and develop knowledge as a strategic business differentiator, and establish it as a core corporate value. Responsible for the design, implementation and leadership of the knowledge process and content, you will work closely with IT and HR to establish a knowledge culture throughout Australia. This is about leveraging structured knowledge as a key enabler, and its conversion to strategic business opportunities. As a knowledge professional with an inspired leadership and team building style, you clearly understand knowledge as an asset to strategic business."

Leaders in business will thus be dealing with a workforce of vastly different skills, both in their disciplines and their levels, with much more cultural diversity. It should be recognised that, whilst Australia prides itself on being one of the world's most culturally diverse nations, dealing with cultural diversity in a domestic environment is vastly different from dealing with such diversity in a number of foreign countries in real time mode.

Apart from this cultural diversity, leaders will have to deal with generational diversity. The day of the Baby Boomers (born 1946-61) will have passed and Generation X (born 1961-81) and Y (born 1981-97) will be centre stage. These generations have very different experiences, attitudes, attributes, and expectations. The challenge for leaders will be to harness the energies of these very different sets of followers. A further complication will be an aging workforce who will not retire in the traditional manner.

A leadership challenge will be to balance the tendency in recent years to work longer not shorter hours, as promised by the seers, with a commitment to family life and a growing need for lifelong learning.

Workforce dynamics will provide some leadership challenges with a substantial growth in the proportion of casual and part-time workers as opposed to full-time. The very nature of knowledge work will create knowledge workers who realise that their intellectual skills and knowledge are their revenue stream, and they will be constantly seeking to optimize that return.

They will become more itinerant and work as contractors, experts, consultants, part-timers, casuals, joint-venture partners, and so on. Today part of the persona of the individual is whom they work for. In the future it is more likely to be, what knowledge area do they work in. It will not be *Who do you work for?*, but *What do you know?*

There will be a move away from the current emphasis on teams towards more one-to-one relationships. And the networked relationships will create new complexities for leaders. Several changes in jobs throughout a lifetime will not only create a new type of worker, it will also create new demands by the worker for increased career support services, such as lifelong learning. Constant training, retraining, job changing and career changes will become the norm in the 21st century. The field marshal's baton in the knapsack will probably remain the only example (outside of the church) of that truism.

There will be many more intrapreneurs as an outcome of businesses seeking more highly-educated and motivated staff, and operating in a global marketplace, which perforce will provide many more opportunities and challenges. One of the biggest impacts will be the effect of the demographic changes the next century will bring. This should not be underestimated and could well be one of the defining issues of the 21st century.

Drucker (1997) believes that "The countries of the developed world are in the process of committing collective suicide." If current trends continue, we shall see effects like the following:

> Italy's population will drop from 60 million today to 40 million by 2050 and 20 million by 2100.
> Japan will drop from 125 million to 55 million in 21st century.
> Australia's population will stabilize around 23 million in 2050.
> In Greece, Portugal, and Spain the reproduction rate is less than half that needed to maintain the population.

> In 2050, not a single European state, including Russia, will match the Philippines in total population.
> In Australia, population share aged 65 and over will rise from 12% in 1997 to 22% by 2031.

With life expectancy increasing and fertility rates decreasing, the population is rapidly ageing. The mix between younger people of prime working age and older people will deteriorate about twice as fast as the drop in population.

The economic impact is obvious with fewer and fewer in the workforce supporting more and more on welfare. However, the knowledge economy will provide a countervailing force in that knowledge-based jobs are not necessarily age sensitive in either content or physical capacity. People will be able to, if they want to, remain a productive member of the workforce for much longer. We are likely to see retirement ages blow out to 75. It also means that economic growth cannot come from workforce growth, it must come from productivity improvements. The competitive edge that developed economies have, and will maintain for some time, is knowledge work and knowledge workers. For example, in the United States there are 12.5 million college and university students in a population 1/5 of that of China, which has some three million students.

The concept of stakeholders will undergo a major rethink in terms of employees of knowledge-based businesses. Today we see the shareholders as the owners of the business and the major stakeholders (in some instances management think and act as if they were). Employees are seen as stakeholders, but one category that can be fairly easily replaced. Those that leave the production line at GM are easily replaceable. The knowledge worker who has just created a brilliant piece of software cannot similarly be replaced as he walks out the virtual door.

## Changes to the Situation

The boundaryless company will become a reality in the 21st century. Barriers between functions, between people, between countries, between suppliers and customers, between levels in the hierarchy, will disappear or be pushed aside. This will be fuelled by the convergence of technologies and the globalisation of business.

In an increasingly global world in which size or critical mass will become more important, there will be a move away from partnerships to corporate structures in the major professional fields of accounting, law, management consulting, engineering, medical services, and similar activities.

In a somewhat contradictory trend, because people and knowledge are the principal assets in the knowledge economy, there will be far more attention paid to these aspects than to structures. Leaders will have to devote a lot more attention to the more intangible aspects of the human condition, such as emotion, attitudes, beliefs, community involvement, social cohesion, and so on.

To be truly successful, leaders will have to establish a seamless union of organisational and individual values. In the same context, concern will need to be extended beyond the employee to the spouse and children. It will be necessary to adopt a much more comprehensive understanding of the over-all environment and to appreciate that the $21^{st}$ century man and woman is a very different person in many respects from the $20^{th}$ century version in their expectations, needs and wants.

Leaders will need to be much more sensitive to human, psychological, cultural and family issues. People will, in a search for a more balanced lifestyle, have a different set of priorities to their forebears, conditioned not only by economic factors, but also by societal change. There will be an increasing focus on the performance of people as a core company asset.

Cultural capital will become the focus of leadership to reflect the importance of people and knowledge. Market forces will continue to drive change, but leaders will have to cope with a market which is global on the one hand, but multi-domestic on the other, in the sense of offering products or services in a variety of countries and cultures. There will be many 'right' ways to do things. Interdependency will increase between teams, as few individuals will be capable of doing or knowing it all.

Without superb management and inspired leadership the likely result is chaos, but of course the true leader thrives on chaos and hence, great opportunities will present themselves. There will be a significant shift in the nature of information in that today most of the information in a firm concerns internal operations, reports on events and activities, progress reports, financial reports and so on. In a much more turbulent and global economy there will be a need for much more information on external events and conditions. Leaders will need to understand more about what is going on out-side the firm to be successful. Leaders will be faced with obtaining the best results from their knowledge resources in a global marketplace. They will have to cope with sudden shifts in their competition. This will require rig-orous methods of gathering and analyzing information from a multiplicity of sources with limited time to respond.

Knowledge is mobile. In a manufacturing economy the means of produc-tion are owned by the firm. In the knowledge economy the means of pro-duction are owned, if not in a legal sense at least in a practical sense, by the individuals and when they move, the production line moves with them.

One of the functions of leaders is to act as the public face of the business. In the networked world there is going to be much less corporate privacy. It will be much more difficult to control the public image.

Associated with this will be a shift away from the dominant shareholder value perspective to a much broader stakeholder view. Who owns the com-pany will become an even more difficult question to answer. Leaders will have to cope with a much more transparent environment where company operations are more open to the public gaze than they have been to date. Leaders will have to learn to turn this increased visibility into an advantage rather than a disadvantage. This will entail using feedback as a mechanism to respond positively to events whether they are favourable or not, and using these opportunities to influence events they can no longer control.

In the next century leaders will be much keener to embrace what Collins and Porras (1994) call the "Genius of the AND" and shake off the oppres-sion of the "Tyranny of the OR". Leaders will recognise that the networked world does give much more flexibility to pursue seemingly opposing or contradictory goals. To have both stability AND change; to be both conser-vative AND bold; to have both low cost AND high quality; to produce short-term results AND have a long-term strategy. This liberation will give leaders even more opportunity to create change, to challenge the status quo, and to adopt visionary goals.

Porter (1998) says that as companies can now source capital, goods, infor-mation, and technology from around the world, often with the click of a mouse, much of the conventional wisdom about how companies and nations compete needs to be overhauled. He sees *clusters*—critical masses

in one place of unusual competitive success in particular fields—as domi-
nating the world economy.

He emphasises the need for continual innovation in today's economy and
the importance of what happens in the immediate business environment
outside companies. The very nature of clusters and they way they operate
will impose greater demands on leaders to perform. For example, he sees
the intersection of clusters providing the stimulus for new businesses. It is
those leaders who grasp these opportunities who will prosper in the new
economy.

## Changes to Education

For Australia, one of the critical challenges in leadership in the 21st century
will be education. This will be important at all levels, but particularly in
post-secondary education.

The social environment is clearly more complex and diverse than we have
previously experienced, with the danger of a substantial "underclass" developing, with limited opportunities to contribute to and benefit from modern
society.

The economic realities of global competition mean that there is little option
for Australian society but to build its competitive strength to sustain living
standards.

There is a need to recognise the new capabilities presented by information
and communications technology. The new technologies offer limited help
in developing the key attributes that business seeks in graduates—communication and interpersonal skills, decision-making and problem-solving
skills, knowledge of work and careers. These can only be developed effectively through a process where social and workplace experiences are inter-
woven with the learning process. That learning process does not stop with
an undergraduate degree, but continues throughout much of the graduate's
career.

Increasingly, post-compulsory education will be called upon to assist with
the career-long accumulation of specialised knowledge and skills. Post-
graduate study (both award and non-award), often workplace-based, is
likely to be much more in demand from individuals and businesses as we
move forward.

In a knowledge economy, education at all levels is important, but particularly post-secondary education. As a nation we cannot expect to be in a leadership position unless our higher education system provides the appropriate platform of skills to compete on a global basis.

Research undertaken for the Business/Higher Education Round Table (BHERT, 1991, 1992) points to the following characteristics of future demand for higher education:

- more workplace-related content in study programs,
- more emphasis on communication, interpersonal and team skills,
- a broad range of abilities, including numerical and economic literacy,
- a high level of professional skill, able to be applied in workplace situations,
- higher education institutions that reach out to provide specialised learning opportunities to employees throughout their careers,
- university teaching and research staff that are experienced across both the academic and business sectors,
- a bridging of the academic and workplace cultures in the design and delivery of post-graduate and research programs, and
- a learning environment that encourages quality, excellence and high ethical and performance standards.

These outcomes will require:

- more emphasis on business/education cooperation and collaboration at all levels,
- institutions that are free and appropriately resourced to innovate and cope with change,
- government encouragement and investment in research that will benefit Australia and Australians.

BHERT's research was recognised and reinforced by an OECD review of tertiary education in Australia (OECD, 1997):

> " the changing employment market is not leading to a greater demand for narrowly-trained specialists but for graduates who can think for themselves, communicate, empathise and work with others, invent solutions and create new possibilities."

In addition there are a number of other aspects which are important for higher educators to grapple with. In the future our students will have to learn the importance of focusing much more on design than analysis. There is a danger in many of our current programs of too much concentration on instilling analytical skills rather than the designing skills that will be much more important tomorrow.

This is somewhat analogous to the misdirected focus in most university education to the search for answers rather than the search for questions. An awful lot of time is spent drilling into our students the solutions, the right answers, the correct approach, the appropriate methodology, and precious little teaching them to think, to question, to search mind and conscience for the new and different.

We will also need to direct attention to the creation of value. The systems and products of a new economy will have to pass a much more stringent test of adding value than when perhaps just adding revenue was enough.

Creativity and the ability to think outside the square are essential characteristics in the global economy. Competition is much fiercer and much more lethal than it was in the good old days. The past is going to be a much less useful frame of reference than it used to be, and certainly the benchmarks will be much more demanding.

The competitive advantages of the past, such as low cost, better quality, or better distribution are going to be displaced by the need for much stronger value creation by way of integrated values.

There will need to be a much stronger focus on externals to the firm rather than internals. Strategy should always have been more about what one's competitors are going to do rather than, as it has been, what can be done internally to reduce costs, expand markets, increase sales, etc. The threats are going to be a rapidly changing environment in which there will be just the quick and the dead.

Complexity has been a feature of business in the past and this will have to be replaced by simplicity. How many people can use 100% of the features on their VCR? In tomorrow's economy, such a product is dead. Someone said every university should have a KISS Institute to instill in students that unless the product or service can pass the KISS (Keep It Simple Stupid) test in the marketplace, it will not compete.

In Australia we are a very risk averse society and universities will discover eventually that today's economy requires a much higher level of risk acceptance. They will discover eventually (apart from a few at the moment) that small business management and entrepreneurship can actually be taught.

In Australia in recent years there has been a strong movement towards measuring competencies in relation to job performance. In essence this is a concentration on how well one can actually carry out a task rather than what is understood about the task. All well and good at some levels, but certainly out of place at the university level, despite the proponents arguing otherwise. Pushing the forefront of knowledge requires understanding not just competency in doing.

There will need to be a radical shift from teaching to learning. The first thing I tell my students is that neither I nor anyone else can "teach" them leadership, but I will do my best to help them "learn" about leadership.

There will need to be a long overdue focus on leadership rather than management. This applies particularly in Australia where there has been precious little attention paid to leadership in the Schools of Management.

Business will become increasingly demanding of what it wants from higher education. It will want to see much more responsiveness from academics to meeting their (business) needs; it will want to see much more relevance in what universities are proposing to deliver; it will want to make sure that what is being delivered is of the highest quality; and it will expect higher education to see it as an equal partner in deciding what to be delivered and how it is going to be delivered. Universities, particularly, will have to reassess many of their attitudes to both education and business to effectively meet these demands.

**Changes in the Process**

Leadership will remain, as it is today, a process of interaction between leader and followers in a particular situation. It will remain, as it is today, the process of actively seeking change, of questioning the status quo, of challenging goals, of communicating and motivating, of articulating visions and energising followers.

It will remain, as it is today, a process of setting challenging goals and getting people to perform beyond their own expectations. But the new environment will impose new demands. The internet-based context in which many businesses will be operating will present new challenges in communication. Inspiring followers in a face-to-face situation is one thing. Doing the same thing via e-mail or a video-conference, with the possible loss of facial expressions, body language, group responses, and the atmosphere of a physical meeting is quite another. Challenging the status quo always poses challenges. Challenging several status quo simultaneously raises challenges of a new order.

Creating and articulating a vision is a difficult enough task under any circumstances. Doing this in a virtual environment, which may change constantly, is for more difficult.

## **Conclusion**

In the 21st century there will be many more firsts in senior leadership roles in Australia than there were in the past century. Australia has for far too long clung to its traditional WASP heritage. One only has to look around in government, in business, in professional associations, in community groups, and in political parties, to see the exclusivity of our leaders.

It was a sad commentary on our sectarian hang-ups when the first question I was asked by the press after I was elected as Federal President of the Liberal Party was whether I was aware that I was the first Catholic elected to that position. I was not aware and to this day have never bothered to check, although I believe that is the fact. My response was that I was not aware, did not care, and it was as relevant as my shoe size. That was Australia in 1990. It has to change. It will change.

There will be far less concern with gender, religion, race, or age in an environment which is global, neutral, virtual and instant. However, people will still be people. They will still need leadership to fulfill their dreams, to realise their ambitions, to achieve their goals. They will still need leaders to inspire them to previously unreachable heights. Those leaders will themselves need to scale new heights.

One lesson we should have learned from the Olympic Games is that PBs (personal bests) are no longer good enough. Leaders will have to set goals based not on historical achievements, but on the best in the world. It is no longer good enough to do 50% better than last year if that will only win the silver medal.

*Whatever changes we see in leadership, be it in the 21st or the 31st century, there will always be one essential unchangeable ingredient to effective leadership, and that is integrity.*

# EPILOGUE

Many times throughout the book I have emphasised the fundamental importance of integrity.

One of my most gratifying reflections is a cover story done by *The Bulletin* (9 October 1990) in which a panel nominated 21 of Australia's most ethical business people. I was one of those named. That gave me a great deal of personal satisfaction.

**As Dwight Eisenhower said,**

> *"In order to be a leader a man must have followers. And to have followers, a man must have their confidence. Hence the supreme quality for leadership is unquestionably integrity. Without it, no real success is possible, no matter whether it is a section gang, on a football field, in an army, or in an office. If a man's associates find him guilty of phoniness, if they find that he lacks forthright integrity, he will fail. His teachings and actions must square with each other. The first great need therefore is integrity and high purpose."*

Jack Welch, Chairman and CEO of GE from 1981 to 2001, and generally regarded as the outstanding business leader of our time, said, "In the end, integrity is all you've got." (Lowe, 1998, p.36).

GE in their booklet, *The Spirit and the Letter*, which they give to every employee, starts with a message from Welch, which in part, reads:

> *"Integrity is the rock upon which we build our business success-our quality products and services, our forthright relations with customers and suppliers, and ultimately, our winning competitive record. GE's quest for competitive excellence begins and ends with our commitment to ethical conduct."* (Lowe, p.70)

In his final television interview before he died on 25 February 2001, Sir Donald Bradman, the greatest cricketer the world has seen or is ever likely to see, and a true sportsman and a gentleman in every sense of the word, was asked if he had to capture in one word what he would like to be remembered for, said without a moment's hesitation, "Integrity".

He knew what was important in life and I can say no more than to urge you to follow his example.  A true leader.

# REFERENCES

Bass,B M (1960): *Leadership, Psychology and Organisational Behaviour*,Harper,N.Y.

Beer, Michael & Nohria, Nitin (2000): *Cracking the Code of Change*, Harvard Business Review, May-June, 2000

Bennis, W G (1989); *On Becoming a Leader*, Addison-Wesley, Mass.

BHERT (1991): Business/Higher Education Round Table Melbourne: *Aiming Higher.*

BHERT (1992): Business/Higher Education Round Table, Melbourne: *Educating for Excellence,*

Burns, James MacGregor (1978): *Leadership,* Harper & Row, NY

Burnes, Bernard (1992): *Managing Change*, Pitman Publishing, London

Collins, J C & Porras,J I (1994): *Built To Last-Successful Habits of Visionary Companies,* Century, London

Conger, J A, & Kanungo, R N (1988): *Charismatic Leadership: The Elusive Factor in Organisational Effectiveness*, Jossey-Bass, San Francisco

Cummings, Thomas & Huse, Edgar (1989). *Organization Development and Change.* St Paul, MN: West Publishing Company.

Drucker, Peter F (1997): *The Future That Has Already Happened*, Harvard Business Review, September-October, 1997

Giuliani, Rudolph W (2002): *Leadership*, Talk Miramax Books, N.Y.

Goleman, Daniel (1995): *Emotional Intelligence*, Bantam

Goleman, Daniel (1998): *Working with Emotional Intelligence*, Bantam

Hage, J (1980): *Theories of Organisations: Form, Process and Transformation*, Wiley, NY

Hickson, David J, Richard J Butler, David Cray, Geoffrey R Mallory, and David C Wilson (1986): *Top Decisions: Strategic Decision Making in Organisations*, Jossey-Bass, San Francisco

Hughes, R L; Ginnett, R C; Curphy, G J (1993): *Leadership- Enhancing the Lessons of Experience*, Irwin Publishers, Boston

Kotter, John (2001): Kotter's Point of View: *5 Degrees of Change-Leadership and Change*, http://hbsworkingknowledge.hbs.edu/kotter

Kouzes, James M. & Posner, Barry Z. (1995): *The Leadership Challenge-How to KeepGetting Extraordinary Things Done in Organisations*, Jossey-Bass Publishers, San Francisco.

Langley, Monica (2003):Tearing Down the Walls, Free Press, NY

Lowe, Janet (1998): *Jack Welch Speaks*, John Wiley & Sons, N.Y.

March, James G and Herbert A Simon (1958): *Organisations*, Wiley, N.Y.

Mintzberg, Henry (1989): *Mintzberg on Management,* The Free Press, NY

Mintzberg, Henry, Duru Raisinghani, and Andre Theoret (1976): *The Structure of Unstructured Decision Processes*, Administrative Science Quarterly, pp. 21, 246-275.

Nanus, Burt (1992): *Visionary Leadership,* Jossey-Bass Publishers, San Francisco

OECD (1997): *Thematic Review of the First Years of Tertiary Education in Australia* - OECD, February 1997

Newman, John Henry Cardinal (1987): *The Idea of a University*, Loyola University Press, Chicago

Porter, Michael (1998): *Clusters and the New Economics of Competition*, Harvard Business Review, November-December, 1998

Powell, Colin L (1995*): A Soldier's Way*, Hutchinson, London

Rae, John (1993): *Delusions of Grandeur*, Harper Collins, London

Senge, Peter M (1993*): The Fifth Discipline; The Art and Practice of the Learning Organisation*, Random House, 1993

Simon, Herbert A (1957): *Administrative Behavior*, the Macmillan Co., NY

————- (1960): *The New Science of Managerial Decision*, Harper and Row, NY

————- (1977**):** *New Science of Management Decisions,* 3rd. ed., Prentice-Hall, NJ

———— (1987): Making Management Decisions: The Role of Intuition and Emotion, *Academy of Management Executive*,1, February, pp.57-64

Viney, J (1999): *Drive- What Makes a Leader in Business and Beyond*, Bloomsbury Publishing, London

Yukl, G (1994): *Leadership in Organizations*, Prentice Hall, 3rd ed.

Zaleznik, Abraham (1992): Managers and Leaders: Are They Different? Harvard Business Review, March-April 1992, pp.126-133

# ABOUT THE AUTHOR

Ashley Goldsworthy is in a unique position to write a book on Leadership. In a career spanning over 55 years he has been CEO of Australia's largest housing and construction company; a retail bank; the Australian Computer Society; Australia's Business/Higher Education Round Table; deputy to the CEO of a large insurance company; chairman of an international construction company; Director of Economic Statistics for the Australian Government; Dean of the Business School at Australia's first private university; one of Australia's first Professors of Leadership; Federal President of the Liberal Party of Australia; World President of the International Federation for Information Processing; director of one of Australia's largest casinos; founding chairman of a university Centre for International Research on Communication and Information Technologies; chairman/director of performing arts companies in ballet, theatre and circus; chairman of several private and public companies ranging across human resources, accounting, financial services, healthcare, computer systems, and vocational education and training; member of the Business Council of Australia, the Australian Science and Technology Council, and the Australian Government Industry Research & Development Board; and Consultant to the Australian Law Reform Commission .

Has published over 140 papers, mainly in IT, and was recognised by his peers by being honoured in 1982 with an Order of the British Empire, in 1991 with an Order of Australia, and in 2003 with the Centenary Medal, and being elected a Fellow of the Australian Academy of Technological Sciences and Engineering in 1994, and the Chinese Institute of Electronics in 1996. In 2005 he was admitted to the Pearcey Hall of Fame for distinguished lifetime achievement and contribution to the development and growth of the Information Technology Professions, Research and Industry.

He has degrees in accounting, business, public administration, science, and theology

CPSIA information can be obtained at www.ICGtesting.com
Printed in the USA
LVOW131516170213

320480LV00002B/590/P